WHEN CHOPSTICKS MEET APPLE PIE

*Cross–Cultural Musings on
Life, Family, and Food*

ANNABEL ANNUO LIU

ISBN-13: 978-1539549406
ISBN-10: 1539549402

WHEN CHOPSTICKS
MEET APPLE PIE

*Cross-Cultural Musings on
Life, Family, and Food*

for
Andrea, Doug, Clif, Tracy
&
Sylvia, Julia, Nathan

CONTENTS

CONTENTS (CONTINUED)

Disclaimer: This is not a cookbook. Anyone following the "recipes" in this volume will do so at his own risk.

Preface

Between you and me, I used to think memoir writing was akin to navel gazing, among the most self-indulgent of human endeavors. All those I, I, Is, ugh. Who needs it?

However, life has a way of changing our minds. After having published eight books in Chinese, mostly collections of literary essays and short stories, I quit writing to care for my ill husband. Little did I know that the hiatus would last seven years and that in three of those seven years I would lose my husband, my health, and my home.

After what seemed like several lifetimes, across the continent in a senior living center, I started writing again, astonishing myself by penning what I had been least inclined to write—a memoir—in English, my second language. What's more, once I started, I couldn't stop. Before I knew it, I had a trilogy.

Why would anyone write three memoirs about one life? Some may even think: *enough already!*

Each of my three memoirs is about a different and significant facet of my life. I wrote the first, *My Years as Chang Tsen: Two Wars, One Childhood*, to tell my granddaughters what I experienced growing up in war-torn China. I was two years old when the Sino-Japanese War started, and fourteen when the Chinese Civil War ended.

The second volume, *Under the Towering Tree: A Daughter's Memoir*, examines my less-than-idyllic relationship with my father, a complicated man who was far more tyrannical than the traditional Chinese patriarch.

My father sent me to this country from Taiwan in 1957 with

the directive that, come hell or high water, I was never allowed to go home. He didn't explain why, and he didn't need to. He believed it was his prerogative to give orders and be obeyed absolutely. Only later did I realize he sent all three of his children, plus a nephew and a niece, to establish ourselves in America, so that he and my mother could eventually join us and escape the clutches of the Chinese Communists.

That was how I came to this country at age twenty-two, fresh out of college, armed with one hundred dollars and a small parcel of textbook English. I had no idea what I had left behind or what my future would hold.

Back home, every morning I would awaken to the sporadic chanting of street peddlers and emerge from my mosquito-net-covered bed, smelling the fragrant scallions of fried rice from the kitchen. A few months later, I opened my eyes in a girls' co-op house in Eugene, Oregon to find my blankets covered with a layer of snow, for I slept by the solitary window (kept open at all times for ventilation) in the attic with thirty American girls. Some of them would already be downstairs in the kitchen, where the sound of chatter and laughter rose with the foreign, and therefore vaguely threatening, smell of coffee.

The smell of breakfast is, of course, a very small part of acclimating to a drastically different culture, but for me food became, and continued to be, a very important part of that struggle. I had taken the food I grew up with for granted, not realizing I was going to spend the rest of my life—now nearly sixty years—craving it and searching for it.

Food, after all, is a metaphor for an immigrant's undying yearning, her perennial reaching for her mother culture. The integration of the new and the loss of the old. The joys and tribulations of living on the margins and straddling two worlds. It's my hope that through this collection of essays, you will see a rather impressionistic depiction of an immigrant's life—*my life*—through the lens of food.

PART I:

Some Facts I'm Not Particularly Proud of

I.

The Most Food-Obsessed People in the World

Take it from me. The Chinese are the most food-obsessed people in the world. I know such hyperbole requires scientific evidence to back it up, but you'll just have to trust me.

To begin with, the Chinese are the only people in the world whose daily greetings, until very recently, involved food. Nowadays, the Chinese typically greet foreigners with *Nihao* (How are you?), but that's a westernized version, not very Chinese at all. If you are Chinese, you don't need to know how people are, you want to know whether they have eaten. Through the ages—at least when I was growing up in China and later, in Taiwan—we never said *Nihao*. Instead, we asked, *Chifan lemei?* (Have you had your rice yet?) or, more to the point, *Chibao lemei?* (Have you eaten your fill?) The implied logic was clear—if you've had enough to eat, you must be doing fine.

By the same logic, having *more* than enough to eat was even better. So being overweight used to be a sign of prosperity, to be envied in others, to be proud of in yourself. When you saw someone you hadn't seen for a while, the typical compliment to give was *nin fafu la* (Gee, you've put on a few pounds!) synonymous with "You've gotten prosperous!" This would make the recipient very happy.

How we greeted one another is, of course, only one of the manifestations of our food obsession. In general, food is of greater importance to us than to people in many other cultures. Nothing can be far from *chi* (to eat). Just before, during, and after a great meal, what do we talk about?

Food, of course.

The Chinese obsession with food has a great deal to do with history. Almost everyone in China loves to tout the fact that we have a 5,000-year culture. (If they don't tout it, they think it.) But few mention that those 5,000 years were under an indefensible political system. The upshot is, until very recently, China was a very poor country most of the time, in most regions. When people are impoverished for thousands of years, they tend to be pragmatic. When they are both destitute and pragmatic, they tend to focus on their most urgent issue—their growling stomachs.

Conversely, during occasional periods and in places of affluence, they tend to overcompensate, like that infamous former first lady of the Philippines, Mrs. Marcos, and her 500 pairs of shoes. When I saw a film with Henry VIII gorging on chicken drumsticks, I was not impressed. In China, the emperor and his queens dined on one hundred exquisite dishes, with the most luxurious ingredients, for every single meal.

Of course the emperor and his queens couldn't possibly *consume* one hundred dishes in one sitting. The kitchen staff, with the eunuchs who waited on the royals, conspired to place their favorite dishes close to them; the rest were just reheated and served again. But count them—there had to be one hundred dishes at each and every meal.

§

Although I have never seen it written or talked about anywhere, I think there is another reason, a more profound reason, that the Chinese focus so much on food.

Confucius.

Almost everyone has heard of Confucius, but not many can truly appreciate his influence on Chinese culture. The "Extremely Sage Departed Teacher," the "Model Teacher for Ten Thousand Generations," whose school of thought has dictated Chinese behavior for the past 2,500 years, readily acknowledged *shi se xing ye*: food and sex are intrinsic to human nature. In other words, they are the two most basic human needs.

At the same time, however, the code of ethics, or *lijiao*, espoused by Confucius, further dictated that the needs of some were more important than those of others. His hierarchy was most rigid and harsh: elder over junior and men over women. Ostensibly, he devised the code to maintain stability in society.

We don't know what happened in Confucius' early life to shape his philosophies. Despite the fact that his mother and his wife were both female, to say he detested women would be an understatement. He didn't just consider them inferior; he was of the firm opinion they were subhuman, fit only to be men's property, playthings, and breeding machines. His famous disparaging remark? *From time immemorial, it's been difficult to get along with women and scum.* On account of his convictions, for thousands of years, murdering your wife was no more a crime than breaking a plate or dismantling a chair. It was no crime; therefore, no punishment was necessary.

One could also argue that Confucius didn't hate women at all. He simply recognized the extraordinary danger of sex, and established stringent rules to contain it by subjugating women. His *three rules of obedience* maintained that a woman had to obey her father at home, her husband in marriage, and her son after her husband's death. In addition, his teaching that it is a virtue for women to be without talent, and his principle of conduct, *no physical contact across the gender line*, kept women imprisoned at home, illiterate and totally powerless.

Because sex, the second basic human need, was repressed for millennia, like water being dammed at one outlet, it inevitably burst forth through the first basic human need: food. Thanks to Confucius, for tens of centuries, half of the country's population stayed home, procreating and pouring their talent and energy into cooking for the male half.

§

I'm not sure whether it's because China is a historically impoverished country, or because of some peculiarity of its people, or both, but the Chinese tend not to discriminate in their choice of food. They eat practically everything, and they are proud of it. Understandably, their food choices can raise a few eyebrows—to say the least—in other cultures.

For example, for years my husband, Sam, and I lived in a

small town in Iowa, where most of the numerous—and I mean *numerous*—Chinese vegetables we had grown up with were unheard of. One evening, a friend had us for dinner and invited us to see her beautiful garden before the meal. We were admiring the flowers when I happened to turn my head and see Sam staring longingly at the pea blossoms.

It was true, those blossoms came in a variety of fetching colors— pink, blue, and lavender, in addition to the usual white. As soon as Sam opened his mouth, however, I realized he had something else on his mind. He told the hostess, "Pick those tender pea shoots and stir-fry them in hot oil. They'll be delicious!"

I was stunned, and the shocked look of our hostess was truly unforgettable, but it didn't bother Sam. He was on a roll, pointing at the day lilies, "And these! You can dry them and braise them with pork or chicken…" He didn't stop until I surreptitiously tugged at his sleeve.

Although the French are famous for eating snails, and people in more than a few countries ingest insects, none of those foods comes close to the exotic fare that some Chinese cook up. Organ meats, chicken claws, dog meat, monkey brains, snakes, and scorpions—not to mention shark fins and swallow's nests—are all edibles, some even delicacies.

Here I must hasten to testify that I have never eaten dog meat (reputed to be truly delicious) or any exotic animals. And I don't personally know anyone who has. I've had soup that supposedly contained shark fin, but what shreds I did find were not impressive. I've never had swallow's nest (the gelatin lining is prized for its digestibility and high protein) and don't feel the worse for it. I mention this to say that, in a country of more than a billion people, there are bound to be some weirdoes doing weird things—but it's the exception, rather than the rule.

That said, the Chinese do have a propensity for gravitating to the unusual as far as food is concerned. When my father was a fisheries executive in Taiwan, at one particular banquet in his honor, the last and most important course was a dish he didn't recognize—which turned out to be duck buttocks. The host assured him duck's tails were a great delicacy.

When my father came home, he looked a bit sheepish—probably the only time I saw him look sheepish—as he described the dish: "A big platter full of...duck...eh...*backseats*!" Concerned that his words might be a bit too euphemistic for us, he repeated with emphasis, "Do you understand? Duck *backseats*!"

We had heard that the other end of the same bird, duck tongue, was a great delicacy—but duck tail? At a time when treating an esteemed guest to a single bird was a great luxury, serving a whole plate of duck *backseats* had to be the epitome of extravagance. When we thought of the host, who went to all that expense only to have it fail to please, we all nodded gravely, "Yes, yes, we understand..."

§

The Chinese proclivity for food obsession—and our inability to do without traditional and treasured ingredients—got both my husband and me in trouble from the very first moment we each arrived in this land of milk and honey. (Although Sam and I both graduated from the same university in Taiwan, we didn't meet until after we came to the States independently.)

As Sam was going through customs in San Francisco, the agent suddenly became agitated when he came upon a pack of white powder in Sam's luggage.

"What's this?" he demanded to know.

"For...cooking," Sam stammered.

He tried to explain that the powder enhances flavor, but he didn't know its name in English. But why would a male college graduate carry some white powder from so far away—*for cooking*? Besides, this young man was so gaunt that he could very well be a cocaine addict.

The officer disappeared into his office with the questionable substance, emerging more than an hour later. The suspect was exonerated; it was not an illegal substance after all. It was MSG (monosodium glutamate) which in 1955 had not yet become famous as the culprit of Chinese Restaurant Syndrome.

Two years later, I arrived in this country on a freighter, landing in Portland, Oregon. The customs agent searched my suitcases and found two small cylinders of *rosong* (dried cooked pork, delicious with rice porridge), a farewell gift from one of my mother's mahjongg friends. I watched helplessly as my precious *rosong* was confiscated on the spot, while the stern-faced agent informed me that U.S. law forbids travelers to bring meat products into the country.

The agent raised no objections, however, to another item in my suitcase—a pair of silver chopsticks with a delicate chain link. My two siblings and I each owned a pair, the carvings on which were intricate and distinctive so one could easily tell them apart. My mother must have tucked mine in my luggage, perhaps with the hope that I would use them the rest of my life and think of home.

Shortly after I arrived at the University of Oregon in Eugene, I moved into a girls' co-operative house. There, in the top drawer of my bureau, my chopsticks reposed unused, for sadly, I had no occasion for them. At the end of the academic year, packing to leave Oregon to eventually transfer to the University of Missouri, I was surprised to find my chopsticks were no longer there. I have no idea what happened to them.

Though my silver chopsticks are gone forever, I've had plenty of opportunities to use chopsticks since. They have been simply indispensable in my life, and decades later even played a role in the momentous occasion when the first Caucasian was about to join our family.

The night before my daughter, Andrea, and her intended were to shop for an engagement ring, an idea suddenly took hold of me and I announced off the cuff: "We're going to start a new tradition. Henceforth, anyone who wishes to join our family must pass a test. They must pick up ten solidly frozen peas with a pair of plastic chopsticks without dropping a single one."

The young man from Kalamazoo, Michigan was unflappable. Doug didn't bother to answer me but turned to Andrea, "Let's postpone our shopping trip tomorrow."

Andrea, of course, was not pleased. "But why?"

"I need time to practice. I wouldn't want to flunk the test and lose face for *you*."

Whoa, wait a minute! If he failed, he would be losing face for *my daughter*? I knew when to concede defeat and waived the test on the spot. Years later, when a second Caucasian (Tracy, my son Clif's betrothed) was ready to join the family, I had learned my lesson and made no mention of a test.

§

China is a huge country, slightly larger than the United States in area. Before the latter part of twentieth century, the vast majority of the Chinese population lived quite isolated due to lack of transportation. As a result, dialects and food varied widely from region to region, in many cases even from village to village. There was, and still is, a great discrepancy of wealth, from the exorbitantly rich to the indescribably poor, and all the myriad shades in between. And as I said before, you eat quite differently when you possess different resources.

The Cantonese, being from a coastal province, were the first to emigrate to the U.S. Many were imported to build railroads and consequently brought poor people's food to America. (This country had to wait to sample the Chinese food of the wealthy, since, generally speaking, those who were well-off tended to stay put, not risking life and good fortune by moving away.) By the late 1960s, spicy food from Sichuan and Hunan, the Southwestern regional provinces, also made its appearance here. Now if you live in a big city, you will find restaurants offering dishes from Shanghai, Fujian, and Lanzhou, to name a few.

I came to this country at age twenty-two. More than two decades in China and Taiwan gave me the opportunity to have experienced—albeit to a limited extent—the variety and magnificence of Chinese food. I developed proper appreciation and respect for the fact that our ancestors, although destitute and beset by numerous calamities in life, were so masterful, so innovative in their effort to create highly enjoyable food from extremely meager resources. How they managed to produce the variety of flavors, textures, and shapes in their meals, is simply astounding. And none of the mind-boggling, mouth-watering fare had any help from Kraft or Uncle Ben.

My family background also contributed, not in small measure, to my own appreciation for food. Both my parents came from upper-middle-class families, but due to two major wars (namely, the eight-year Sino-Japanese War immediately followed by the four-year Civil War) they had to live with a lower-middle-class pocketbook. Because of babies, those wars, and my father's strenuous objections, not necessarily in that order, my mother never put her hard-earned medical degree to use. To her profound regret, she never had the opportunity to practice medicine. After the Sino-Japanese war, she spent the rest of her life, true to Confucius' principle, as a gracious hostess, masterminding splendid meals for my father and his friends.

My father was from Yangzhou, an important historical city known for its culture and cuisine. (Many famous dishes from Shanghai actually originate from nearby Yangzhou.) A connoisseur of food and a gentleman, my father followed Confucius' tenet that *gentlemen must stay away from the kitchen* to the letter. This did not, however, prevent him from holding forth in glorious detail about proper food preparation. I gained some rudimentary knowledge from his frequent impromptu lectures on the subject.

As of this writing, I have spent more than three quarters of my life in the U.S. Obviously, I'm no longer one-hundred-percent Chinese. However, having spent my formative years in China and Taiwan, I can never be one-hundred-percent American either. Behavior formed in my early upbringing often comes off as eccentric or obstinate, causing me to stick out like a sore thumb in certain places, on certain occasions. By necessity, an immigrant is a hybrid, prone to being awkward, inconvenient. In my case, I have always seemed to be drifting outside the American mainstream, alone and unmoored.

In many aspects, being a hybrid has made my life immeasurably richer, but also incredibly more difficult and complicated— especially regarding food, that first basic human need. For I find that no matter how many years I have spent in this country, my Chinese palate remains the most consistently obstinate, imperious, and least adaptable organ in my body.

2.

More Power to That Snake

Although food obsession seems to be predominant in the Chinese collective genes, in my case, perversely, a love of eating fails to translate to a love of cooking. Except when I'm hungry, I prefer not to think about food at all. There's always something more interesting or more pressing to occupy my thoughts. Unfortunately and inconveniently, I get hungry several times a day.

Even worse, after I married and had a family in the 1960s, I found myself having to cook for not one but two, not two but four—and the other three almost always grew hungry before I did. That was when I realized I had a problem—two paradoxical, contradictory, conflicting, incompatible traits of my personality: I love to eat but I hate to cook. The Chinese refer to women like this, rather derogatorily, as *haochi lanzuo*: Love to eat, but too lazy to cook. For me, one trait was always at war with the other, with the lazy part often gaining the upper hand.

These two traits have always ruled my life, and I can't change them any more than I can alter my shoe size. In other words, I'm constantly pulled in opposite directions.

I was about fifty years old when I read that when a large four-foot snake swallows a small rat, it doesn't need to eat for the rest of the week. I don't know who else might have read that tidbit or how they reacted. But I'm telling you—I became extraordinarily jealous of that snake. I thought, *Wow, for a whole blessed week he's satiated, not having to worry about the next meal.* I'm only one foot longer than he is, but I have always had to eat three meals a day, which comes to twenty-one meals per week—twenty more meals than that lucky snake. And my children had to eat more often,

9

especially when they were shorter than four feet. As a wife and mother in this country, in the days before the advent of fast food and take-out, the responsibility of serving at least three meals a day fell squarely on my two not very broad shoulders.

By the time I turned fifty, by my calculations I had cooked approximately 27,375 meals in my life. By any definition, when you've engaged in so many battles, you are a veteran—and I was a seasoned (pardon the pun) veteran in the kitchen.

And what did this kitchen veteran fear the most? What would instantly send shivers down my spine and trigger my impulse to run and hide? The question I heard every single day: "What's for dinner?"

The cruelest irony of all is that even now—well into my fourth quarter-century, living alone with no one to ask me the dreaded question any more—I still have to ask myself the same question and try to come up with an answer at least three times a day.

Occasionally I try a volunteer system: I opened the freezer door, and whatever falls out is the volunteer. If nothing does, I encourage a would-be volunteer by poking the contents a little. Something usually obliges.

Of course these days, at my age, I am constantly exhorted to live every day as if it were my last. Oh, really? Then I wouldn't have to do laundry, pay taxes, or refill my prescriptions. And I wouldn't need to cook. I would just take a taxi to a fabulous restaurant for a sumptuous dinner with the most decadent dessert, and to hell with cost, indigestion, or gaining weight!

Come on, we all know it won't work. For who knows which day is truly our last?

Instead, I have devised two simple rules that I follow religiously. If there's a chore I can postpone until tomorrow, I won't do it today; if there's something I can indulge in today, I don't wait until tomorrow.

§

When I search my background for the reason I have such fear and loathing for cooking, I must admit it has something to do with the first twenty-five years of my life.

Until I left home, I was quite lucky in terms of food. Labor being comparatively cheap in China at the time, we almost always had a maid and a cook. (We even had our maid with us when we fled Shanghai to escape the Japanese soldiers and American bombing at the end of the Sino-Japanese War.)

I never had to cook and was never required to be in the kitchen. I remember one summer vacation during my college years in Taiwan, when I was reading the Chinese translation of *The Count of Mount Cristo*—a big book with several volumes. Shortly after breakfast, before I finished reading one volume, lunch would be served. Before I had a chance to digest my lunch, dinner would be on the table.

It didn't escape my mother's attention that I was preoccupied with my book and couldn't care less about the food. She shook her head and sighed, "Four dishes and a soup, and you're not interested. You'd be incredibly lucky if you got four dishes and a soup every meal the rest of your life."

My mother, as almost always, was right. If she had gone into business as a fortuneteller, she would have made a fortune. The day I left home, my days of four dishes and a soup were gone forever.

To her credit, my mother did try to train me to cook before I left for the United States. In fact, she began by "teaching" me to make the bed.

My mother excelled in everything she did. She also had an unusual way of teaching. She didn't show me how to make the bed or give me any verbal instructions. No, she went straight to the heart of the matter. She gave me a test—to make *her* bed.

I'm ashamed to say that up to that point in time, I had never made a bed. A Chinese bed was different from an American bed. We didn't have bedspreads. Making a bed simply meant folding the quilt and piling a pillow on top. However, I had never done that either, because it was the maid's job.

My parents' bed was the only one in our house that had the whole works—sheets, blankets, and bedspread (cotton chenille with multi-color horizontal stripes)—a typical American bed.

Unfortunately, I'm not good with my hands, never was. I was good at turning the pages of a book, but couldn't neatly turn her bedspread to keep those horizontal stripes straight to save my life. After struggling clumsily and desperately for a good amount of time, all the while aware of my mother's cool gaze behind my back, I suddenly blurted out, "The more I try to *babajiejie* (please), the more I *jiejiebaba* (mess up)!"

My mother laughed; end of my bed-making lesson.

Next came the inevitable cooking lesson. My mother had always been very successful in training our succession of family cooks. Those men or women already knew the basics when they came to work for us. She only needed to give verbal instructions on her specialty dishes, or correct what they didn't do right. She seldom needed to go into the kitchen. When she trained *me*, she didn't go into the kitchen either. She simply decided I should do one basic dish. If I could master that and apply the experience to other dishes, I wouldn't have to starve in the foreign country. She decided I should cook braised fish. "Just fry the fish and add wine, soy sauce, and other seasonings and simmer till done. What could be easier than that?" she asked rhetorically.

On the appointed day, I walked into the kitchen with some trepidation. The cook had thoughtfully done the preparation, and there it was—a whole fish, cleaned of its innards, de-scaled, ready to go into a large wok of smoking hot oil.

I was young and intrepid at the time—comparatively speaking—but I sensed it wasn't going to be as easy as my mother put it. For one thing, the fish looked pretty naked without its usual condiments. For another, I was going to have to pick up this fish, cold, slimy, and dead—its eyes staring dully at me—with my bare hands. For yet another, that wok of hot oil didn't look awfully friendly…

While I was mulling over the situation, the cook was apparently thinking, too. He thought that I wasn't quite up to the task. He thought the oil was terribly hot and couldn't wait. Rather than wait for me to gather my courage to throw the fish in the oil and get both of us splattered and burned, he thought the best solution would be for him to take it in his own hands and gently slide it into the wok.

That was exactly what he did. One kind deed led to another,

he finished cooking the fish, and I carried it on the platter to the dining room. My mother, none the wiser, thought the fish tasted "adequate" and pronounced my training complete.

Less than a month later, I was on a freighter bound for Portland, Oregon.

It was early September. Most of the approximately thirty passengers on that freighter were students, and I met a girl who was also on her way to the University of Oregon. Naturally we decided to be roommates after we landed. She was a few years older and more experienced in the kitchen, so she cooked and I washed dishes.

Things went swimmingly for a while. But life is like that—when things go swimmingly, there always comes a catch. It turned out that the University of Oregon required all incoming foreign students to pass an English test. I passed, but my roommate failed and transferred away soon after.

My heart was heavy as I entered the empty apartment the evening after bidding her goodbye. My only friend in this foreign country was gone. And more importantly, she had paid half the rent and cooked all the meals. What was I going to do now?

I opened the refrigerator in the hope of finding some leftovers, and lo and behold, there was a huge bag of sandwiches sitting there! Apparently she had made them for her trip and had forgotten to take them. I survived on those sandwiches for a few days as I searched for a solution to my problem. I decided to move into the girls' cooperative house next door—where they had a full-time cook.

The following fall, I transferred to the University of Missouri. Again, I shared a room in a private home with a fellow graduate student from Taiwan. As in the symbiotic arrangement in Oregon, my roommate cooked and I washed dishes. Again the deal fell through, for a different reason: she fell in love with a classmate and was no longer around at dinnertime. Left to my own devices, I improvised by making a big pot of porridge (two cups rice and ten cups water, boil till thickened, add soy sauce and half dozen eggs and stir well). It usually lasted me several days.

I survived on porridge until the end of semester when I moved again into a girls' cooperative, where we were served lunch and dinner.

By the time I graduated from the University of Missouri with a master's degree and boarded a bus for New York, I was twenty-five years old and had miraculously managed to survive without having to cook any real meals.

Except for one fateful evening, when I had no choice but to prepare an "authentic Chinese dinner" for an American family of five.

3.
Rock 'n' Roll Eggs

Shortly after I had moved into the girls' cooperative at the University of Oregon, the Foreign Student Advisor's Office set me up with a "friendship family" to foster cultural exchange and ease my transition. The Smithsons invited me for dinner a few times, and I found their hospitality and interest in everything Chinese heartwarming.

When Mrs. Smithson asked me to cook them "an authentic Chinese dinner," I couldn't say no. With those five pairs of eyes looking at me so expectantly, how could I tell them that I was almost twenty-three but had never learned to boil water?

I went back to the co-op house that night feeling as desperate as a non-swimmer forced to dog paddle her way across the English Channel. Fortunately, my mother had had the foresight to provide a life buoy—a cookbook she had slipped into my suitcase before I left home. I spent a good part of two nights leafing through the book, fairly dog-earing it in the process.

To plan one dinner from a 109-page cookbook with nearly 150 entrées should not have been such a difficult task. In this case, however, I had some unusual considerations.

First, I had to eschew all dishes requiring ingredients that, according to the author, could be purchased "in any market in Shanghai." For the same reason, delicacies such as eels and squab had to be scrapped. Next I chopped off all main courses that required cutting meat, whether to cubes, slices, shreds, or dices, for the simple reason I had never used a knife in my life. For good measure, I also deep-sixed anything that called for deep-frying. My single experience with that wok of hot oil was enough.

Not too many candidates survived that ruthless pruning process, it's true, but among the remaining recipes, the entrée with the fewest ingredients, called *Yaogun Dan*, literally "Rock 'n' Roll Eggs," caught my attention.

At the time, a typical Chinese cookbook only gave a list of ingredients and a vague description of the process, no measurements or photos. This volume was no exception. For Rock 'n' Roll Eggs, three lines said it all. The author described it as an *easy* and *interesting* dish from a city famous for its cuisine, Suzhou. All one needed to do was to drill a tiny hole (the book didn't specify with what tool; perhaps it was public knowledge) in each egg and empty its contents; mix with soy sauce, salt, sugar, minced scallions, and ground pork; return the mixture to the shell and steam the eggs until done.

I figured I could handle that.

I had probably seen people crack an egg before in my life, but I had never physically held a raw egg in my hand. If learning how to crack an egg should have been my cooking lesson number one, drilling a tiny hole in it would have qualified as the final exam.

Unarmed with such vital insight, I discovered on the appointed day that eggshell tends to crack at the slightest pressure, and that a jagged little hole soon gives way to a large one. Before I knew it, the shell of the first egg gave out, allowing the Smithsons' gleaming kitchen counter and floor a generous taste of the uncooked dinner, while the five members of the Smithson family waited to be fed.

Switching frantically from a small knife to scissors yielded similar results. After nearly half of the two-dozen eggs suffered the same fate, even Mr. Smithson, who had been watching television in the living room, became involved. Observing his dinner in jeopardy and his wife, grim-faced, busy wiping the counter and floor, he volunteered to rush out to buy another dozen.

There was, however, another problem the cookbook hadn't mentioned: The white and yolk, which had previously fit perfectly in their shell, after being beaten vigorously and joined by the other ingredients, became the genie that wouldn't go back in the bottle. Mrs. Smithson solved the problem by throwing the excess in the garbage. Who could blame her after what the mixture had done to her kitchen?

The cookbook specified using "sturdy paper" to seal the holes "securely." Since it was before the age of Saran Wrap and I had no clue what paper to use, I decided to leave those gaping holes alone. Why bother to seal them? The eggs would be steamed in a few minutes, I reasoned. Would we need to worry about dust falling into the holes?

Now that all the eggs were nice and full, I heaved a sigh of relief and proceeded to clean their exterior with a damp towel, a nice final touch of my own improvisation. The Smithson's four-year-old daughter Debbie, dropping in to check on the progress of dinner, giggled when I told her that those eggs were getting "a sponge bath." I even had time to steal a glance at my watch—it was an hour and half past our designated dinnertime.

Mrs. Smithson brought me several Pyrex pie plates. As soon as I began to transfer the eggs from their nestling place of the egg cartons to the plate, I realized why they were named "Rock 'n' Roll Eggs." Did they ever rock and roll! Before I could right one humpty dumpty, another would fall, spilling its runny guts all over the plate. This modern-day Sisyphus had her hands full, scooping up the mixture to refill the eggs, one by one.

Quick to sense something had gone seriously awry, Debbie began to cry, screaming, "Mommy, Mommy, I don't want Chinese food! I want a peanut butter sandwich!"

It's too painful to recount how those eggs, after countless sponge baths, managed to get on the Smithsons' dinner table, set with polished silver and fresh flowers and aglow with candles, in honor of the feast.

Suffice it to say that Debbie cried again because her mother wouldn't let her add cream and sugar to the "rice pudding." Debbie was right. My first attempt at cooking rice had yielded a dish that was indeed like pudding.

Years have gone by since that horrendous night. Whenever I thought about it, my cheeks would burn, my palms would break out in a cold sweat, and I would feel ashamed and apologetic all over again. The poor Smithsons! They probably did eat peanut butter sandwiches before bed, and they probably never tried

Chinese food again.

As for me, I developed a rather severe case of PTSD—Post-Traumatic Stress Disorder. For the next almost sixty years, I tried, although not always successfully, to keep cooking at arm's length.

Nietzsche once said (perhaps he said it many times, but since Nietzsche was his usual biting self, *ouch!* once was quite enough): "Bad cooks—and the utter lack of reason in the kitchen—have delayed human development longest and impaired it most." I don't mean to sound paranoid, but I have a sneaking suspicion that he was speaking about the likes of me.

4.
That Big, Heavy Wok

Speaking of brilliant quips, some wit once observed that a woman, no matter how extensive her wardrobe, is always in need of just one more outfit. As a writer, I am ready to testify that, to write anything worthy of readers' attention, I can always use more, too—more hard work, better ideas, catchier turns of phrase.

The same is true of being a parent. Whatever qualities and skills you might have, you are invariably caught short. In time, I found parenthood to be the single most difficult job, far more challenging than being a writer or a woman, which are no picnic, either. In my old age, I've found that aging is even harder, the toughest work I have ever undertaken.

But let's not jump ahead; let's talk about parenthood. For such formidable work one would think nature would have devised a stringent system to screen out the unqualified. Reality is obviously otherwise. I attained parenthood long on ignorance of its ramifications, and short on the right stuff for handling the job.

On each of the two occasions Sam and I brought our precious bundle home from the hospital, we were awestruck by the responsibility of rearing this fragile and vulnerable little being.

Our awe soon gave way to shock. In both cases we discovered that, despite their physical helplessness, our children had minds and wills of their own. When their desires didn't coincide with ours, they never hesitated to let us know. As tiny and tender as their skulls were, they were never timid about locking horns with us.

In each of those early confrontations, one would assume that we, as parents, enjoyed every unfair advantage. We were bigger, stronger, and more knowledgeable than they, and we were two against one. But we had one significant weakness: we wanted to do our conscientious best. We had to tread carefully for fear that, with one false move, they might be affected adversely for the rest of their lives.

To cite two trivial examples: once when Clifton was around two, I cut his fingernails a bit too closely by mistake, and he became forever fearful of nail trims. As a young adult, Andrea once made the mistake of allowing me to trim her bangs when she didn't have time to go to the hairdresser. She claimed afterward that my clumsy efforts made her look dumb. I, who had cut her hair throughout her childhood!

If parenthood is not a piece of cake, the conflict of dual cultures certainly made it infinitely worse. Our major confrontations always centered on that theme.

The first one involved language.

Like the vast majority of first-generation Chinese-American parents, Sam and I very much wanted our children to be bilingual. We took care to speak to Andrea (our firstborn) only in Mandarin, and were pleased that she was fluent at age two. Smug in my naiveté, I thought our good work was done; nursery school would simply serve to round out the rest—the English portion.

A few weeks into nursery school, Andrea's speech began to resemble the Christmas tree in our family room: its trunk and branches were still genuine, but more and more foreign objects began to dangle on them. When she was telling me about her day at school, I observed with alarm that the Chinese "tree" was covered entirely with English "ornaments." While the "ornaments" sparkled, I could see the "tree" itself was withering, soon to suffer the fate of all Christmas trees after the holiday season. I felt compelled to interrupt. "Um…wait a minute. Would you mind telling Mommy this in Chinese?"

"Okay. But Mommy, what's 'field trip' in Chinese?"

Hmm…this was a bit tricky. Here, if the teacher takes the students out of school to go any place, it's a field trip. In Chinese, if you take a hike, it's *yuan zhu*; but if you go to a museum, it becomes *can guan*.

"Well, where did you go?"

She looked at me in dismay. "The pet shop. What's 'pet shop' in Chinese?"

She got me again. In all my years in China and Taiwan, I had never seen or heard of a pet shop. It was an idea as foreign as "family room," for which there was, at that time, no ready translation either. I had to improvise. After having to stop frequently for reinforcement of her newly-inadequate Chinese vocabulary, Andrea announced in frustration, "I don't feel like telling it any more."

That was potent ammunition indeed. Speaking Mandarin and mother-daughter communication were mutually exclusive? I was quick to capitulate, not realizing that with one concession, one step backward, it was all the way downhill. Our dream of bilingual children was lost forever.

§

Around the same time, we had another confrontation—at our dinner table. The same little tyke, who previously ate my food with gusto, first began to reject all stir-fried dishes, then anything that did not resemble standard American fare.

To be sure, almost all immigrant parents have faced the same situation with their American-born children. Many of my Chinese-American friends solved the problem by designating the center of their dinner table as a demilitarized zone, serving hamburgers and hot dogs at one end and steamed whole fish with shredded mushrooms at the other.

While this practice prevented conflicts, it also brought on complications of a different sort. Often, while the parents were enjoying their dried squid stir-fried with pork and thousand-year-eggs with tofu and cilantro, a cry would arise from the junior end of the table: "What's that? Y-U-C-K!"

I wondered if by tacitly allowing our children to thumb their nose at our food—a vital part of our heritage—weren't we permitting them to look down on Chinese culture in general? Not to mention the additional work of producing two different dinners every night. For someone who found cooking one dinner a big chore, preparing two was unthinkable.

More importantly, should we allow a mere toddler to decide what she would or would not eat for the rest of her life? To close the door on Chinese cuisine and to subsist henceforth on a diet of American processed food?

Furthermore, if we caved in on the food front, wouldn't we be tying our hands on future issues involving melding with the mainstream versus following one's good judgment?

For these considerations, legitimate or not, I tried every way to dissuade Andrea from her chosen path. I reasoned with her, sweet-talked her, bribed her, threatened her, spanked her. Sam even tried to force-feed her. All to no avail.

In desperation, I changed my tactics during lunch one day by asking her a question in a casual and non-threatening manner. "Why aren't you eating? Don't you like the food?"

Circumspect even under duress, yet as obstinate as ever, she countered, "I'm *not* hungry."

"In that case," I said, "you don't have to eat. And since your appetite has been rather poor lately, we'd better not spoil it for dinner with any snacks between meals."

As she was excused from the table without the usual coercion and scolding, looking relieved and pleased, I added helpfully, "You may drink as much water as you like."

The kid who was not hungry became inordinately interested in food by two o'clock, casting frequent and plaintive looks at the refrigerator. By half past three she could stand it no longer and asked for crackers. That afternoon was a challenge for us both. While I struggled to enforce my new "no snacks" rule, she alternated temper tantrums with fruitless trips to the kitchen. When dinner was finally served, she tried to maintain her tough stance, but her hunger got the better of her.

The tug of war was over in three days.

Decades later, during one of our visits to Andrea's home shortly after she was married, instead of eating out as we usually did on such occasions, she decided to cook us a Chinese dinner. As she and Doug labored side-by-side in the kitchen, I noticed she had a well-used wok.

"Oh, that," she said, tossing a handful of bok choy into the wok,

"I bought it in Chinatown after moving out of the dorm in my sophomore year. I remember lugging this big, heavy wok all the way on the train and back to my apartment in Berkeley..."

The dinner they cooked that night was delicious, and she went on to become an accomplished cook in several different cuisines, including Chinese.

5.

You Cook Your Meals, I'll Cook Mine

One night many years ago, Sam and I invited a few new friends over for dinner. Shortly after sitting down at the table, we heard from the kitchen the sound of running water interspersed with whistling.

Our guests were shocked to the point of leaving the table to investigate. They found Clif, a high school senior at the time, washing pots and pans in a practiced and cheerful manner.

"How much do you pay him?" they demanded to know.

"Not a penny," I confessed.

Their shock giving way to envy, our guests sighed almost in unison: "How lucky you are to have a child so capable and willing to help!"

I smiled. The fact is, luck had nothing to do with it.

When I was growing up in China and later in Taiwan, I often heard the saying that America is a paradise for the young, a battlefield for the middle-aged, and a graveyard for the old. The birth of my children certainly brought home the truth of the first part of this saying, together with the sad realization that we Chinese-American immigrants are getting the short end of the stick. Having grown up in a society where children were totally subservient to their parents, we had become parents in a land where the reverse seemed to be true.

The Chinese children of my time had to obey, respect, and honor our parents. We were also considered family resources, to be tapped whenever and however our parents deemed fit. Children of the poor had to work in and out of the home, while those of others, with paid household help, were constantly commanded to study hard to glorify the family name and increase the family fortune.

While I found the Chinese way too authoritarian, the American way seemed overindulgent. The majority of American parents would rather work themselves to the bone than make any demands on their children, the rationale being—and I have heard it often—"They are only young once." So the able-bodied young are not given any responsibilities except having fun.

If a mother is sick with the flu and tries to enlist the help of her daughter to make dinner, the girl might respond: "Why can't we just order pizza?" Or if a man develops a back problem and asks his son to mow the lawn, the boy, busy playing video games, might say, "Thirty bucks isn't enough for the trouble. How about $45?"

Paying children for doing housework seems peculiar to me. We are members of the same family. If I do it for free, why should they be paid? I think it deprives them of the pride and pleasure of being contributing members of the household.

Long before my two children were tall enough to reach the counter, I bought two step stools and *invited* them both to *help*. Too young and unsophisticated to see through my ploy, they accepted my invitation with enthusiasm.

Much of what they did in the beginning, of course, was counter-productive. Training the little ones to help with housework required a great deal of tact, patience, and, most of all, work. (In fact, they were not impressed with my tact; I learned later that they saw my attempt at teaching as criticism. But I wasn't aware of the difference in opinion at the time.)

Many times I had to redo the work surreptitiously, and numerous utensils were broken in the process. But what the heck! It was analogous to paying tuition. One day their training would pay off and they would be of real help.

Little did I realize that before that day dawned, they'd start to rebel. When their help grew from occasional fun as guest artists to regular appearances, Clif was first to protest. "My buddy Jimmy has never touched a rag in his life," he declared with great feeling. "Rob has never washed the dishes, and Steve doesn't even know where the vacuum is in his house. No kids I know ever do a lick of work around the house. Why am I stuck with all these chores?" He was eight years old.

My mother was visiting us from Taiwan at the time. She had always taken a dim view of my making such liberal use of child labor, and had never been reluctant to let me know. She took the opportunity of Clif's impassioned protest to give me a meaningful look: *I knew you'd get into trouble.*

Surrender and let all the tuition investments go down the drain? Heaven forbid! I tried to save the day by reasoning: "Suppose someone gave us a cake, and Daddy and Mommy ate it all, leaving you not a crumb. Would you think it's fair?"

"Of course not!"

"You get to share all the good things, but not the work. Is that fair?"

"But I'm a kid!" He almost started bawling. "Kids aren't supposed to work! Other kids don't!"

Sooner or later, every child learns to use the formidable phrase "other kids..." I didn't know who these "other kids" were, but they were allowed to stay up late, eat dessert before dinner, and generally get away with murder. It's a trump card that works like magic in most households, but failed in ours because this parent possesses a heart of stone.

"Other kids are not my kids," I reminded him. "Besides, it's dangerous to follow other kids. If they steal or jump off a bridge, would you do the same?"

"And because you are *just a kid*," I added sweetly, "I haven't asked you to shop for groceries or fill out our income tax forms."

Unable to refute my impeccable logic, he walked away looking sullen. After school the next day, he came back to argue his case again: "I've thought about this carefully. We all eat dinner, but only us kids have to clean up the kitchen. This is unfair."

I reminded him that I was the only one who did the cooking.

"That's what I thought you'd say," he replied calmly. "From now on, I'll do my own cooking and clean my own dishes."

His face still retained some baby fat, his eyes still resembled crescent moons when he smiled, but he felt ready to assert his rights. I didn't know whether to laugh or cry. He said he had thought the whole thing through. I could teach him to cook the same meals.

"Are you sure that will be easier and you won't end up with more work?"

"Absolutely sure!"

I decided not to dissuade him.

Pleased with his newly gained freedom, he invited his sister to join him in his fight against parental tyranny. Being three years older and correspondingly wiser, Andrea refused. Thus she spent the afternoon as always, reading a novel and practicing the piano, while her brother worked with me in the kitchen. Under my tutelage, he cooked rice, washed, cut, and stir-fried vegetables, sliced and braised meat, so busy that he had to turn down several invitations from his friends to go out and play.

When dinner was finally ready, he was quiet and ate little, looking wistful and preoccupied. After the cleanup, he approached me with a pained expression. "My tummy hurts," he said.

"Why?" I was surprised. "I didn't see anything that could have upset your stomach."

After a slight pause, he suggested rather off-handedly, "I want to do my own cooking. But since it brings on tummy aches, maybe I should...uh...just eat with you guys."

I answered, also trying my best to sound casual, "That's okay with me."

A few months later, Andrea tried a different strategy: "Cindy gets $15 every time she cleans the stove for her mom. I think you ought to pay us, too."

I marveled, "What a great idea! I pay you when you work for me, and you pay me when I work for you. I'll charge $5 to drive you to piano lessons, $15 a week for washing and ironing your clothes, $4 for cooking a dinner, $2 for packing your lunch... Oh, yes, and when you were a baby, I nursed you and changed your diapers many times a day. I'll give them to you wholesale..."

I was happily adding up the numbers when Andrea abruptly stopped me. "Forget it," she said. "Let's not worry about paying each other."

"That's okay with me," I replied.

6.

Ode to Laziness

I don't know precisely when I acquired the notoriety of being a lazy cook. The fact was first brought to my attention when a friend asked me casually, "What did Andrea cook for you when she was home from college last week?"

The implication of that inquiry was not lost on me. It's like being asked, "Have you stopped beating your wife yet?" If the answer is yes, you admit you have been guilty of domestic abuse. "No" is worse, meaning you're guilty *and* still at it.

In other words, whether or not my daughter cooked for me when she was home, my reputation as a lazy mother had already been firmly established.

Americans believe that money is the root of all evils, but a Chinese proverb declares unequivocally that *lust is at the top of 10,000 evils*. I'm certain that laziness cannot be far behind money or lust. For example, my culinary laziness once nearly caused my mother to—oh, well, perhaps I should tell you the whole story:

In the mid-1970s, our family of four spent the academic year in the San Francisco Bay Area while Sam was a visiting professor at the University of California at Berkeley. During that time, my mother came to visit us from Taiwan. One day I was going to make egg fried rice for lunch and found I was a bit short on cooked rice. (You need cold, cooked rice to make fried rice.)

That didn't bother me. Some frozen peas would add bulk and lend color and more nutrition to the dish.

As luck would have it, I was out of frozen peas. This had also happened before, and I had a ready solution. I grabbed a loaf of the city's famous sourdough bread to dice, sauté, and add to the rice.

(I was always innovative in cooking, ahead of my time, if I may say so myself. In modern parlance, I practically invented fusion food.)

My mother happened to be in the kitchen at the time. She saw what I was doing and turned pale, demanding, "Surely, you're not going to serve bread and rice in the same dish?"

I tried to appease her. "It may look a little weird, but it does taste good. I'm adding some great San Francisco sourdough bread, and the kids have always liked my fried rice that way."

Solemnly, my mother drew herself up to her full height, and for a moment she looked taller and more imposing. She declared sternly, "It doesn't matter what kind of bread you use. You are making slop for pigs. Your kids may not know better, but I for one, am not about to put that stuff in my mouth!"

That was the end of that particular fusion dish that day, but not the end of the story as far as my mother was concerned. For years afterward, every time we were together, she would bring up that incident to illustrate how unbelievably lazy and sloppy (pardon the pun) I was. And that if she hadn't stood her ground, I would have fed her pig slop! From then on she was forever on her guard in my home. Every time I tried to employ some laborsaving device, she would shoot it down immediately with her four-word verdict—*it won't taste right*.

On one occasion, she recited for my benefit detailed instructions on the preparation of mung bean noodles. Heretofore I had always rinsed the bunch under the faucet and added them to whatever dish I was making. I still do. The only tricks are to have enough liquid to allow the noodles to soak up and to time the other ingredients carefully so that everything in the dish is done at the same time. Undercooked, the noodles are hard and inedible; overcooked, they dissolve into nothingness—you'd never even know they are there. Ideally, they acquire the flavor of whatever company they keep and contribute succulent texture, as only mung bean noodles can.

My mother was in the early stage of Alzheimer's disease at the time, but she gave a perfectly lucid thirty-minute lecture, step by step, on how to prepare the noodles prior to cooking. Mentally counting the steps involved, I soon gave up, thinking, *My God, why torture those poor noodles to death before you even throw them in the pot?*

Needless to say, I never learned the *proper* way to cook mung bean noodles, and I avoided using them when my mother was present.

§

Though some of my creative *fusion* dishes met with success, I admit there were more moments of poor judgment, motivated by laziness on my part. For instance, the incident of the poultry bag.

Perhaps it is public knowledge in this country that when you buy a whole chicken or turkey, you will find in its cavity a bag containing the neck, gizzard, liver, and heart. For someone new to the culture, it can be quite a surprise, even an unpleasant one.

Luckily, I had been forewarned about the organ bag by Sam's former roommate, who was greatly embarrassed to come upon a paper bag containing the chicken's innards in the middle of a dinner with a bunch of guests looking on. Needless to say, he had never cooked before and thought he could throw a chicken in the pot with some soy sauce and impress his friends.

Though saved by this fellow's snafu, I encountered my own version of the problem when we lived in Denmark in the early 1970s, where Sam served as a visiting professor at the University of Copenhagen. Since I have the undesirable habit of trying to cut corners whenever I can, I took for granted that Danish chickens didn't come with an organ bag. It *was* a foreign country, wasn't it? Why bother to search the chicken's cavity?

Imagine the consternation halfway into our family dinner when the bag of organs appeared. What's more, the bag was not of wax paper but plastic, and only half of it remained—the other half being inconveniently and imperceptibly one with the soup.

A serious discussion ensued. Should we throw away the soup and go hungry? There was no takeout food to be had. Or should we simply take a chance and dig in? Sam was never one to vote for hunger, so he decided that we should go ahead. I worried for days afterward, fearful of untoward effects on the whole family from plastic poisoning.

§

In general, I have a bad attitude towards anything I *must* do and don't particularly want to do, including making dinner. In addition, I soon discovered that if I served dinner at six o'clock, whether I began to cook at four or five o'clock, the outcome would pretty much be the same: in thirty minutes, the fruits of my labor would be gone, and I would have to start all over again the next day. So why begin early?

Of course, starting too late presented other problems. High heat was usually necessary, often resulting in burned food and hands. When I made a pot of soup, the stovetop typically got the first taste. Dishes that required more time got too little, and I would be serving a portion to appease the family appetite, then shuttling between the dinner table and the stove for the duration of the meal.

Unfortunately, in my younger days, in addition to cooking three family meals a day, I also had to entertain. I certainly had mixed feelings when friends, especially Chinese-American ones, invited us for dinner—my anticipation of the pleasure of a good meal was invariably tainted by the worry of the inevitable obligation to reciprocate.

It is the Chinese custom to serve at least ten courses for a dinner party. How I suffered, watching multiple meticulously prepared courses coming to the table one after the other, the hostess cool and calm, every strand of hair in place, her beautiful dress and her kitchen both remaining spotless. I would be gripped by a deep feeling of inadequacy and shame.

A solution finally came to me by chance. One evening, Sam had a dinner meeting and I was fretting about what I would eat. (Our kids were both in college by then.) The leftovers in the fridge didn't look too appetizing. Before going out the door, Sam suggested, "Why not cook something for yourself?"

Later when he asked me what I had, I gloated, "The same leftovers, but not until eight o'clock! And you know what? Everything tastes better when you are *really* hungry. In other words, all it takes is time. Time will *turn water to chicken broth*!" (This was the advertising slogan for MSG when we were growing up.)

Now that I possessed the secret, I was dauntless. I would fulfill my long overdue obligations by inviting guests for a six o'clock dinner and serving at eight. After two hours of drinks and very few hors d'oeuvres, everyone would be starving and easy to please.

On that day, I waited till half past seven to get into the kitchen, when guests started stealing glances at their watches. I was extremely hungry myself.

Was my blood sugar too low? How could I have spilled the sauce I had prepared for the shrimp on the salt-water duck? I was trying to salvage the situation when the wok—*Jesus Christ*! The oil in the wok had caught fire! While the sound of talk and laughter wafted from the living room, and the smell of burnt oil and black smoke wafted from the kitchen, this Don Quixote was bravely fighting the windmill—alone.

Murphy's Law says, "Anything that can go wrong, will." Thoreau said, "The mass of men lead lives of quiet desperation." The evening, needless to say, proved them both correct, and I never tried the same trick again.

§

Perhaps laziness is hereditary, or at least contagious. Whatever the cause, it certainly affected the other members of my family. When Clif was in first grade, one morning he seemed to be groggier than usual, with his jeans on backwards. I told him, "Better run upstairs and change, or you'll be late for school."

"That's all right," he assured me. "I'll just walk backwards today."

Over the years, Sam always took a dim view of my inclinations. In his retirement, he even took to gnawing noisily on crackers to signal that he needed to eat. It didn't matter that I was in the middle of writing. Why couldn't he make his own meal?

One day, he vented his feelings on the subject by announcing out of the blue, "Behind every successful woman, there's a starving man."

The nerve! Did he miss a single meal on account of my writing? As a matter of fact, since his retirement, I had lost a great deal of writing time every day because I had had to cook him lunch. Peanut butter sandwiches simply wouldn't do.

I retaliated: "Buddy, you got it wrong. Behind every *un*successful woman, there's a man who's constantly complaining of starving."

7.
Love, Marriage, and a Deadbeat Turkey

Some cynic once said love is a seed catalogue with beautiful photos of blooming flowers, while marriage is your own back yard, chock full of weeds and wilting plants. In life, often—if not always—there exists a sizable gap between ideals and reality. In my case, it translated to what I *wished* to serve for dinner versus what I could realistically produce every night.

At times, bridging that gap called for creativity. In other words, whenever I faced a formidable problem in the kitchen, I would try to solve it in an unorthodox way.

And sometimes I got lucky—as I did for one Thanksgiving dinner.

A Thanksgiving dinner must feature a turkey, but roasting that bird was never an easy task for me. Although I had done it for forty years, I was only called to action once a year. The twenty-pound turkey was inevitably tough and dry after roasting for several hours in the oven—no matter how many times I basted it, taking the back-breaking bird in and out of that blasting hot oven. To be palatable, it had to be eaten with a lot of gravy, like swallowing water to make pills go down. And I was not particularly fond of the greasy smoke during the roasting process, or of cleaning the oven afterward. I thought, *for God's sake, I'm almost seventy years old—I deserve a vacation from this.*

I did come up with an easier way. After all, as they say, when the going gets tough, the tough get going.

First, I went to the local health food store and chose an organic, fresh, free-range, eleven-pound turkey. Then I bought a large oval crock-pot. I was quite proud of myself that the two fit as if they

35

had been made for each other. Since it was years before brining came into vogue, I heated some salt with Chinese peppercorn and planned to rub the bird inside out with the warm mixture and let it sit in the refrigerator for a few days before cooking.

But before I could apply the salt mixture, I realized I had a problem.

If a twenty pounder is considered a mature turkey, an eleven-pound one is a teenager, and this particular youngster was a free-ranger, which meant that it got plenty of exercise in life and built a lot of muscle. The bird fit in the crock-pot all right, but its breast was so impressive that the glass lid wouldn't close—it kept flopping up and down, like a teeter-totter.

A Chinese satiric aphorism says: "Trim the feet to fit the shoes." In this case, the solution seemed to be obvious and reasonable—to knock the breastbone till it caved in.

We often hear that exercising stops bone loss and prevents osteoporosis. That free-range turkey certainly proved the point. With both hands, I held tight to the handle of a heavy kitchen cleaver, summoned all my energy, and dealt several savage blows with the back of the knife. The turkey didn't yield a whit, but someone behind me began to laugh: "Are you by any chance trying to tickle the turkey?"

Well, since my man of the house thought he was more capable, let *him* try.

From tickling to slapping and whacking didn't bring any progress, but my husband was not in the habit of conceding defeat. He went to the garage for a heavy-duty hammer, the one he used years ago for chopping firewood.

One strike with that Paul Bunyan implement elicited a deep moan.

Holy Moses! The turkey came alive! All my hair stood on end, and I was ready to flee, when I caught a glimpse of our hero's fiery red face—the moan had not come from the pot.

The Chinese like to ridicule a weakling for not having "the strength to tie up a chicken." Here was a man without the strength to beat up a dead turkey. But I recognized the seriousness of the situation immediately—"Stop...please! We'll think of something else. It's not worth a heart attack!"

Despite my tugging at his sleeve in a desperate attempt to stop him, he merely turned a deaf ear, gritted his teeth, and kept pounding. And that poor young turkey! In life, it had to scrounge around for worms; in death, it suffered brutal beatings. The bird was in and out of the crock-pot seven times before Sam finally succeeded in closing the lid.

The Chinese have another saying (the Chinese have a saying for everything under the sun): *when a child is beaten, it's the mother's heart that suffers the pain.* After the turkey was whipped, it was the guy who administered the beatings who hurt all over, and had to rest in bed for three whole days.

Three days took us to the day before Thanksgiving. I rinsed off the salt-peppercorn mixture, added water, and simmered the turkey for a night and a day. And voila! Even the white meat was tender, flavorful, and smooth as silk, sliding down my throat like a prayer. And the clear broth… ah…the broth was to die for. (Someone almost had!)

For a more festive touch, I had cooked some shrimp wontons and added them to the soup. Our children and their respective spouses thought it was an interesting and unusual Thanksgiving dinner.

Before I finished gloating over my success, an article appeared in the *Los Angeles Times* about people employing various creative devices to prepare food.

Riffing off the Polish saying that fish, to taste right, must swim three times (in water, in butter, and in wine) a New York stockbroker made his fish swim a fourth time—in his dishwasher.

To serve Salmon in Cilantro Sauce, he would tightly wrap the fish in foil with olive oil, wine, cilantro, and various other seasonings and place it in the dishwasher. From the wash cycle to rinse to heat, it took fifty minutes, while he served drinks and relaxed with his guests. When the dishwasher stopped, the fish was ready, turning out extraordinarily tender and delicious every time.

The same article reported a lady who tried to up the ante by making *dishwasher lobster* for a group of friends. Unfortunately, when the machine entered the heat cycle, the lobsters started to complain. Their grievances grew to such a pitch that everyone stopped talking and all eyes were fixed on the dishwasher...

Before the age of pre-packaged triple-washed spinach, another lady was preparing spinach salad for seventy-five guests. She placed the washed spinach in a clean pillowcase, stapled it shut, and let the air fluff cycle of her clothes dryer do the rest.

Then there was the innovative flight attendant who used her hotel room coffeemaker to heat up tacos. She also roasted a chicken using the heat from her car engine during a drive from Dallas to Houston. She proudly proclaimed afterward, "It was great, much more tender than baking it in the oven."

The following year, before I could cook up another inventive method of preparing a turkey, our Chinese supermarket in San Diego started taking orders for pre-roasted Thanksgiving turkeys.

Thank heavens! We never had to beat a dead turkey again.

8.

My So-called Repertoire

Don't snicker, but I did have a culinary repertoire of sorts. As far as cooking is concerned, I must confess my intentions have always been dishonorable—to skimp, cheat, and get away with as little work as possible. For example, I have sprinkled soy sauce, sesame oil, and chopped fresh scallions on deli sliced roast beef and passed it off as a Chinese cold dish.

Like a naïve country girl who would time and again fall for no-good city slickers, I have always been seduced by short recipes— preferably one-step recipes, two or three steps at the most. After all, that was why I chose to make that infamous Rock 'n' Roll Eggs—because the recipe was brief and sounded easy.

And I especially favored recipes with few ingredients. Although mankind has been out of the hunting and gathering age for quite a while, gathering ingredients still involves a bit of work. Years ago, a friend—bless her heart—gave me a "Thirty-Minute Cake" recipe, guaranteed not to require a minute more. She was triumphant the next time she saw me: "Pretty easy, wasn't it?" I stared back at her with resentment. "Are you kidding? It took me more than half hour just to find the recipe!"

And I didn't have the heart to tell her that I was totally incapable of following any recipe. I always tried to skip a step or two, omit or substitute an ingredient or two. Before you knew it, the dish had turned into a different animal altogether.

Allow me to go back in years, when I first began developing my repertoire. After leaving Oregon and prior to starting at the University of Missouri, I traveled to Iowa to stay with my older brother Charley for the summer. The first weekend after my arrival, he made egg dumplings to celebrate our reunion.

Like me, he didn't know how to cook when he left home. My mother didn't even bother to train him, probably assuming he would soon find a wife to cook for him. It didn't happen, however. After receiving a master's degree from Montana State, he began his PhD studies at Iowa State. There, he joined a group of graduate students, also from Taiwan, each responsible for cooking dinner for the whole group one day a week.

The first time Charley's turn came, he made steamed eggs, the only dish he knew how to make. You beat a bunch of eggs, add water and some salt, and steam. (Strangely reminiscent of my Rock 'n' Roll Eggs, but much less ambitious.) The other fellows in the group saw the dish and and burst out laughing. Several of them were, as a matter of fact, excellent cooks. They took him in hand and taught him a thing or two—including egg dumplings.

Of course I was no stranger to egg dumplings. At home, however, they usually made their appearance in a hotpot, together with a variety of other goodies. I had never thought they were anything special. But this time, having suffered serious Chinese food deprivation for nine months *and* having subsisted on rest-stop hamburgers on a three-day bus journey from Oregon, I found those egg dumplings utterly irresistible. I've never had "manna from heaven," but those egg dumplings seemed to come close.

The drawback is they are very labor intensive. You start by beating many eggs. Then, in a skillet, make a small crepe about two inches in diameter, spoon in the ground pork filling—seasoned with wine, soy sauce, fresh chopped ginger, and scallions. Before the top of the crepe is set, fold over into a small turnover. Cook slightly and set aside to be braised later with cabbage, ideally napa cabbage. Since timing is paramount, you make one dumpling at a time.

It took Charley a good part of the afternoon to make those egg dumplings, but not many of them got put aside to be braised that day. Under the guise of tasting, I gobbled them up as soon as they were out of the skillet, despite his protest that the pork filling inside was not fully cooked and I might contract trichinosis.

I liked them so much, you'd think that egg dumplings would be number one in my repertoire, right? Wrong. Nothing that takes that much work was going to find its way into *my* kitchen. Instead, I devised a much easier method—by making a batch of large crepes, evenly spreading the pork filling on each, rolling them up, and braising. Presto! Egg dumplings assembly-line style. I named them, appropriately, Egg Rolls.

Every American knows about egg rolls, but in truth the so-called egg rolls in America have no eggs whatsoever—a misnomer. But the Chinese do have spring rolls, which have far better fillings and paper-thin skins. (The feat of making the wrapper skin for spring rolls, by smearing a piece of very elastic dough on a hot skillet and simply peeling it off, always looked like magic to me.)

What the Chinese call egg rolls are baked, sweet and crunchy, much like Pepperidge Farm Pirouettes rolled wafer cookies, except without the fancy chocolate hazelnut filling.

My Egg Rolls, however, were sliced into inch-thick pieces and laid flat like miniature cake rolls, with their braising sauce drizzled on top. If I were feeling ambitious, which was not often, I would sauté some fresh spinach to dress up the dish. I served it the first time I entertained after getting married. A great success, it became a staple in my repertoire.

Next to Egg Rolls, another dish that I simplified to fit in my repertoire was Stuffed Fish with Ginger and Scallion.

Nowadays, even I find it hard to believe, but there was a brief period of time when I was besotted with cooking. Sam was working at IBM's Research Lab in Yorktown Heights, New York, and we were invited to many dinner parties, which we then had to reciprocate. I decided it was a good time to master the culinary arts.

(It was not the only period in my life that I was seduced by illusory hope about food. Years later I subscribed to *Bon Appetit*, until I realized the magazine was my glass ceiling, through which I could glimpse all sorts of tempting, mouth-watering goodies but never had a chance to taste them. They were simply out of my league.)

One day I recalled that my mother sometimes served stuffed clams. Stuffing those big clams with the same filling I used for my Egg Rolls would surely make a more interesting and impressive dish. And let's face it—it saved the trouble of making those large egg crepes.

On the day of the dinner party, however, I came upon an unforeseen hurdle: the clams were so tightly shut that I couldn't pry them open to insert the filling to save my life. How had our cooks at home done it? I had no clue. In desperation, I dropped them into a pot of boiling water. It did the trick but presented an opposite problem: how to close them back up after they were stuffed. I could have sworn my mother served them shut. The guests were ringing the doorbell while I frantically searched our small apartment for strings to tie up the clams…

I don't remember what happened next—I guess I don't want to remember. The hassle of looking for something to tie the clams left me so traumatized that I never made the dish again. Years later, I finally devised an easier adaptation by putting the filling between fish fillets, sandwich-style. Our friends, both the Caucasian and Chinese ones, were impressed.

Another easy item in my repertoire is a dish I call Shanghai Duck: Drop a defrosted whole duck into a pot (not forgetting to remove the organ bag, of course). Add one-third cup each of cooking wine and thick soy sauce, a few anise seeds, bring to a boil, then simmer for four to five hours till the meat practically falls off the bone. During the last hour of simmering, drop in a couple of rock sugar pieces (the Chinese call them *bingtang,* "ice sugar"). They will thicken the sauce, lend the duck a nice shine, and round off the taste. I always drained off the fat and served the duck whole. It's also nice to sauté some fresh vegetables for garnish. As you can see, it can't get much easier than this.

One evening, however, an unexpected extra ingredient got added to my Shanghai Duck.

One of Sam's former PhD students had come to dinner. Harold was famous for his wit and humor. Once, at a physics conference, he and Sam went to a comedy show in the evening. Harold started bantering with the comedian and got more laughter and applause than the standup—to the point that the guy rushed offstage to grab a notebook: "Please…would you say that again?"

At our house that night, Harold was in his usual form. We were all laughing uproariously, especially Sam. Sam had a way of clutching his abdomen while laughing, as if he was suffering from a bellyache. This time he laughed so hard that he almost fell off the chair. As soon as the laughter died down, there came a sound in the sudden quiet: "Ba—da."

Of course I heard it. But before I had any idea what it was and where it came from, I preferred to pretend it wasn't there. Harold, however, wouldn't let me. "What was that?" he demanded.

Everyone fell silent, all eyes searching for the source of the sound. There went "Ba—da" again, with Harold pointing to a drop of water landing on the back of my Shanghai Duck.

Ay-yi... In the seventeen years we lived in that house, only once did the second-story bathroom faucet leak. It had to be the night we had a guest, the water sliding down the dining room chandelier and onto the back of the Shanghai Duck, one drop at a time...

Even Harold, who was never at a loss for words, was speechless.

§

Steamed fish was another favorite in my repertoire. Lightly salt any kind of white fish fillet or whole fish in a large, shallow microwavable dish, then sprinkle with cooking wine and light soy sauce. Arrange shreds of fresh ginger, thinly sliced ham, and shiitake mushroom on top of the fish. (If Chinese ham is unavailable, Virginia ham or Prosciutto will do nicely.) Cover and microwave until almost cooked. Sprinkle chopped scallions and drizzle hot oil evenly on the fish (any vegetable oil except olive oil, as the latter has too strong a flavor that would clash with the delicate flavor of the fish). The hot oil should make a nice sizzling sound. Cover and return to microwave for one minute and serve. This was as close to a one-step dish as I could get.

Of course I couldn't always prepare one-step dishes, but I did try my best to cut corners whenever possible, especially when meat was involved. I don't mind cooked meat, but I hate to handle raw meat, not to say putting a knife to it. I have managed to serve eight-course dinners without cutting raw meat. In fact, if a baby had been born on the same day I last cut raw meat, he or she would be middle-aged by now.

Speaking of middle age, I went through a period of time when I became increasingly concerned with fat intake—particularly animal fat—and invented a couple of vegetarian dishes: namely, stir-fried split peas with oyster sauce and a spinach sandwich.

For the peas, rinse one package of split peas, soak overnight, and boil until tender. Drain the excess water and stir-fry the peas in hot oil in a large wok. Add salt and oyster sauce to taste and mix well. The good thing about this dish is that it will last you a few days.

For the sandwich, heat frozen chopped spinach in a microwave, squeeze out excess liquid and mix with mayonnaise. Sprinkle with black pepper if desired. Toast some whole grain bread and…well, you know how to make a sandwich.

I was quite proud of my innovations until I happened to mention the spinach sandwich to a relative. Unfortunately, I caught a glimpse of the incredulous and rueful look on his face—*How low can your standards be? It's too pathetic for words!* I understand. No self-respecting Chinese would let her cooking deteriorate to such an intolerable state. His look so unnerved me that I haven't had a spinach sandwich since.

§

I have no idea how and when my life fast-forwarded from middle age to old age. It seems as if overnight I became as perishable as the *candle in the wind and frost on the grass*, as the Chinese would characterize it. In this highly transient stage, I realize that I've never been, so to speak, "the master of my fate and captain of my soul."

Until I left for America, my father had dictated everything in my life, large and small. Thereafter, he still tried to exercise firm remote control, with varying degrees of success.

In marriage, while Sam was no tyrant like my father, his temperament and schedule, nevertheless, held considerable sway over my options, and his profession determined where I lived. Our children each came with a new and different set of dos and don'ts.

Now that I'm alone, ostensibly free to live as I please, I find I am unwittingly saddled with a new master—my aging body. He decides where I must live (in a retirement community), what I'm allowed to eat (an ever shrinking list), and what I can or can't do.

Ever more unforgiving, my new master constantly jerks my chain, showing me who's the boss. His orders are strict and exacting, allowing no reasoning, negotiation or evasion. If I cheat or disobey, my punishment is swift and severe. There is no court of appeals. Thus these days, sadly, I've been reduced to my master's most obedient slave, carrying out his wishes, all the while meekly mumbling, *aye, aye, sir, on the double, sir.*

One late, merciful gesture from my master, however. Performing any task, including cooking, has become a long symphony, allowing much needed, meaningful pauses between movements.

Although my cooking style has gone back to that of the Stone Age, and I still frequently and shamelessly resort to what my mother called "pig slop," I have one dish that never fails me. Whenever life goes off track, whenever my *fusion* food is too hard to stomach, I can always eat...a big bowl of chocolate ice cream. Amen.

PART II:

In Pursuit of a Good Meal in the Sticks of America

9.
Of Waitresses and Shrimp in Lobster Sauce

When I was in third grade, every Wednesday afternoon we would spend two hours in class writing an essay, from a topic our teacher assigned on the blackboard. Whatever the topic, I almost always began my essay with a Chinese cliché: "Time is like an arrow; sun and moon are like shuttles." I wasn't the only one using this cliché, and our teacher didn't seem to mind. But the truth was, I had no clue what those words meant. At that age, time seemed to stand still, like an old and sick snail, moving only with great reluctance and difficulty.

I don't know when time really became an arrow, and sun and moon indeed functioned like shuttles, changing me from a grade school student to a graduate student in a foreign country.

My transformation was unspeakably abrupt, drastic, and painful. I had been treated like a grade school student throughout my life, even after I had graduated with a law degree from National Taiwan University, the most prestigious university in the country. Up until the time I left Taiwan, I was closely supervised in every activity, had to return home immediately after school each day, and was never allowed to make any decisions on my own.

Less than a month after graduation, a few months shy of the age of twenty-three, I was put on a freighter and shipped to America to begin my life as a graduate student in journalism at the University of Oregon in Eugene. I found myself in a vast, foreign land, where I knew not a single soul except my brother Charley, who was two thousand miles away in Iowa. I had to fend for myself and make critical life decisions when I had absolutely no experience in either. In addition to homesickness, language barriers, and academic pressures, I lived and worked in the cheapest place I could find—a girls' co-operative. I also did some babysitting on the side to supplement the check Charley sent me every month. My father never sent me a penny, for he assumed Charley would support me with his research assistantship. And, lucky for me, Charley did.

And there was the culture shock; I was, in fact, constantly aghast. I came from a country where college students of the opposite sex sat in the same classrooms for years without showing any recognition of one another. In the States, complete strangers, including those of the opposite sex, said hello to me in the street. Some even asked me how I was. But they didn't seem to want to know because they walked right on by without waiting for an answer. People called me *dear* and *honey*, but they didn't know me at all. Outside the co-op before the ten o'clock curfew, couples clung to each other as if their very lives depended on it. They had no shame!

But what shocked me most of all was American food. The cooperative, Rebec House, had a full-time cook, and I had looked forward to enjoying the meals. In my mind, American food was the same as what we in China referred to as *Western food*, which I held in high esteem, for it represented something rich and exotic, beyond imagination, unlike the run-of-the-mill fare we had at home.

I had only sampled *Western food* a few times during my first ten years of life, when we lived in Shanghai. Going to a so-called Western restaurant was a huge and luxurious event, and we were fortunate enough to have had that experience only once. But among other delicacies, the dainty, delectable curry turnovers we had still stand out in my memory. Then there was the delicious Western confection, called "Princess Snow White"—a vanilla ice cream bar thinly coated with crunchy dark chocolate. In third grade, I occasionally splurged, with my tiny allowance, on a small French baguette to devour stealthily in the school restroom, where I wouldn't have to share my treat.

When I was a child, my mother liked to tell me about a special rice dish in the famous White Russian restaurant on Avenue Joffre, the most fashionable street in the French Concession of Shanghai. (In case you are wondering, concessions in China were born from the unequal treaties the country was forced to sign with various foreign powers. These enclaves were conceded to the sovereignty of respective foreign powers. Unbound by Chinese law, they had their own police, and in some cases, even a small military force. They were, in essence, miniature countries within the host country. Shanghai had two: the French Concession where my family lived, and the International Settlement, joint concessions of the United Kingdom, the U.S., and Japan.)

"When I was carrying you, I couldn't keep anything down," my mother told me. "The only food I enjoyed was a rice dish at this famous White Russian restaurant. It had tomatoes, onions, beef, and I don't know what else—absolutely delicious. I tried to train our cook to make it, but it didn't come close. So I'd go to that restaurant every day, ordering the same dish…"

She was in a rare nostalgic mood. "So you see, you grew up on that dish."

"Did you ever get tired of it?" I asked.

"Never."

"Then how come you don't eat there anymore? And how come I've never been there except in your tummy?"

My mother gave me a look as if to say, *what a dumb question!* Though I was just a small child, I should have known we could no longer afford a meal in a foreign restaurant because of the war.

Perhaps for the love of that Russian dish, my mother learned to make *borscht*. She called it Russian soup—*luosong tang*. It was more like a stew than a soup, with chunks of beef, potato, tomato, onion, and cabbage. Over the years, it managed to retain its allure in our family, to the extent that decades later, my children observed that whenever my family members gathered, we would cook, you guessed it— *luosong tang*.

With this tiny, precious parcel of experience with *Western food*, I arrived in Oregon, moved into Rebec House, and immediately encountered cottage cheese. It looked suspiciously like crushed chalk mixed with water. I thought someone was playing a trick on me and refused to put it in my mouth. (Years later, when I learned that President Nixon—the most powerful man in the world, who could have anything he fancied—loved cottage cheese with ketchup, I was past being shocked. I had been in this country a while at that point.)

The idea of a salad was foreign enough. Many Chinese won't even touch anything raw or cold, considering it unhealthful and uncivilized. Shredded raw carrots mixed with raisins? It simply boggled the mind.

The worst offender was the hot dog. Of course, I had heard of hot dogs; I just had no idea what they were and how they looked and tasted. All my life I had held sacred the exotic, mystical, sophisticated *Western food*, and there it was—the hot dog, the very antithesis of my idea of refined fare.

Unfortunately, my unhappy encounters with the hot dog didn't end in Oregon but followed me to the next girls' co-op at the University of Missouri. (The lure of cheap room and board again being impossible to resist.)

Our "housemother" at Rochdale House, unlike the grandmotherly one in Eugene, was a bubbly, small-town eighteen-year-old. This newly-married teenager, who had the duty of devising the menu for the house, seemed to be unusually fond of hot dogs. Her young husband, our "housefather," was fond of lolling on the front porch. On the days when Rochdale House served hot dogs for lunch, which was two or three times a week, he would take it upon himself to warn me by yelling "HOT DOG! HOT HOG!" as soon as he spotted me from a distance. I would turn around and return to the library.

Our system worked well, except that at lunchtime many students were on the street, and I became self-conscious about the way they looked askance at me. I pleaded with our housefather, "I truly appreciate your warnings, but the trouble is, everybody on the street now thinks my name is *Hot Dog*." So after that, he would wave both of his hands to signal instead.

It didn't take me long to realize that there were more than 150 million Americans in this country at the time, and *they* liked American food just fine. It was my Chinese palate that was the problem.

It's a problem I share with almost every Chinese immigrant I know. Because we can't outgrow our palate and our obsession with Chinese food, our lives in this country seemed to perpetually revolve around Chinese restaurants—from the first years entering through the back door to wash dishes or wait tables, to later settling down in a house in the suburbs and walking through the front door as customers.

We may have different politics (don't talk Chinese politics with a Chinese or a Chinese-American!), and we may be Americanized enough to justify being derided by our countrymen back home as a bunch of "bananas" (yellow on the outside, white inside). But for daily sustenance or occasional restaurant meal, we share one thing in common—we prefer Chinese food. For Chinese expatriates, our perennial longing is for the food we grew up with.

My life has followed the same trajectory for the last nearly sixty years. When I arrived at the University of Oregon, I met two fellow graduate students from Taiwan who were working as waitresses in a Chinese restaurant in town. I always found it apt that the word "waitress" in English sounds like *weiqusi*, "aggrieved to death" in Chinese, and their experiences, indeed, proved they were aggrieved to death:

"The chef sure has *something else* on his mind."

"That dirty old man showed up today and tried again to kiss me."

"I got home at midnight and instantly passed out on my bed, with my coat and apron still on."

I knew I wouldn't do well as an "aggrieved to death"—I didn't have the stamina—so I chose to babysit instead, for the children of the Chinese restaurant owners. At fifty cents an hour, it paid far less than waitressing, but featured a significant benefit. Late at night, when the restaurant owner and his wife returned home, tottering from fatigue and emanating a strong odor of grease that quickly permeated the whole house, they never forgot to bring back several takeout boxes of food for me. Starved from my failure to adapt to the co-op food, I found those egg rolls, barbecued pork, and fried rice—standard Chinese-American chop-suey-joint fare—wondrously delicious, memorable to this day.

After my studies, I went to work in New York City, got married, and moved to an apartment in Mt. Kisco, some forty miles north of New York City in Westchester County, an area totally innocent of Chinese restaurants. On weekends, Sam and I would make our pilgrimage to the city, where we discovered *Baishui* C.B. Fish on the Chinese menu.

It was no secret that Chinese restaurants in big cities practiced an apartheid system of two menus. They still do. When a non-Chinese walks in, he is handed a menu in English, with items the owner thinks Americans prefer, such as Sweet and Sour Pork, chow mein, and egg rolls. None of the stuff Americans are unfamiliar with, especially not anything, God forbid, that might scare them away. On the contrary, if an Asian comes through the door and speaks Chinese, he is given a Chinese menu, with dishes not found on the American menu. Even the same dish is made differently, that is, to the Chinese taste.

Baishui C.B. Fish was always on the Chinese menu at our favorite restaurants. Even then, New York City boasted numerous Chinese restaurants, and competition was fierce. When Chinese restaurants tried to compete, they didn't offer anything unusual to attract customers, nor did they try to improve the quality of food, décor, or cleanliness. Typically they cut prices and copied each other. If one restaurant offered *Baishui* C.B. Fish, every restaurant had to put it on the menu.

Baishui literally means white water—not the kind one can go kayaking in, but just plain water. Ironically, the dish clearly contained no water, and the sauce, complete with wine, soy sauce, and thinly shredded fresh scallions and ginger, wasn't plain either. And what was C.B. fish? At that time, all New York Chinese restaurant waiters spoke the Cantonese dialect and very little Mandarin; asking them got us nowhere. But the fish was always excellent—tender and tasty.

Later we learned C.B. fish was actually sea bass, a fish abundant around the Atlantic coast at the time. We also learned that typical Cantonese-style steamed fish was slightly salted whole fresh fish steamed over boiling water for approximately seven minutes, and doused with the aforementioned seasonings and cilantro. Perhaps the first restaurant owner who put this item on his menu didn't know how to convey the idea of "steamed sea bass" and figured *Baishui* (white water) C.B. Fish was close enough.

Years later, after we moved away and came back to visit New York, we noticed *Baishui* C.B. Fish was history; it was no longer on any menu. Sea bass had probably become too expensive, so Chinese restaurants offered steamed whole flounder instead.

§

The first time I made the acquaintance of Shrimp in Lobster Sauce was also during our years in Westchester County, in a Chinese restaurant in Poughkeepsie. It was the only dish that stood out in my memory that day.

One would think Shrimp in Lobster Sauce would contain some lobster. Not so. Just as the so-called Fish-flavored Pork uses the same seasonings for cooking fish, Shrimp in Lobster Sauce was stir-fried shrimp with the same sauce for stir-frying lobster. I wouldn't go as far as saying it was a great dish, but it was better than the rest of the mundane Chinese-American restaurant fare. Later I learned that it was a favorite of many American customers.

What was in the lobster sauce? One story goes that at a popular Chinese cooking class in New York, when it came to Shrimp in Lobster Sauce, many Jewish-American ladies in attendance were aghast to discover there was actually ground pork in the sauce, and they had unwittingly enjoyed something explicitly forbidden. What was worse, now that they knew, they could never order that dish again.

The moral of that story is, the pursuit of knowledge may be beneficial, but is not without its risks. The story also goes that the teacher learned an important lesson—he substituted ground beef for pork, and peace was on earth again. Word spread among the Chinese, and subsequent cooking teachers never committed the same blunder. Even Chinese restaurants began to use ground beef in their lobster sauce. (A word to the wise. Nowadays with ground chicken readily available, its mild flavor would be a better substitute than beef.)

Another moral of the story: flexibility is required in the process of adapting to a different culture. Sometimes it's necessary to alter one's authentic cuisine to cater to the prevailing custom and taste. (Gosh—I don't believe I actually said that! But let me hasten to add that alteration should only be attempted with the specific purpose of improving the dishes, not to corrupt them beyond recognition or render them inedible.)

Our regular weekend jaunts to Chinese restaurants in New York City resulted in Sam acquiring a bit of a reputation among his non-Chinese colleagues at IBM Research Lab. For the sake of efficiency, he started keeping a file of index cards, recording each worthy Chinese dish on a card, with English on one side, Chinese on the other. Before going to the City, his friends would line up to borrow his cards. Three years later, when Sam accepted a teaching position from his alma mater and we left New York for Ames, Iowa, those most sorry to see him go were the regular card borrowers.

They were devastated to lose their access to up-to-date information on Chinese restaurant menus, but our problem was far more serious. As far as Chinese restaurants were concerned, we were moving from the best place in the nation to one of the worst.

10.

Hello Again, Ham and Peas

When we arrived in Ames, a small university town, at the end of November 1964, winter was just beginning, embracing the whole region in a deep freeze. But the reception from the physics department was surprisingly warm. The chairman led the way in welcoming us, followed by the senior professors, then others. In all, we were invited for dinner at a different faculty member's house every night for a solid two weeks.

Iowa is an agricultural state, ham being one of its major products. The first night I encountered a humongous ham on the chairman's dinner table, I was duly impressed.

The Chinese like to deride some of our fellow countrymen for "finding even the moon in America larger, rounder, and brighter." I've never compared the American moon with the Chinese one, but I will testify that American ham is indeed much larger than its Chinese counterpart. I was also surprised to see that it was pale pink, in contrast to the deep red of the Chinese version.

The chairman carved a huge piece, more than half an inch thick, and placed it on my plate. He was ready to carve me another piece when I stopped him in time: "I think I'll wait…perhaps later…"

I was wise to have declined the second piece. The ham was warm, but its taste left me cold. It was soggy, as if it had been injected with plenty of water, and its texture seemed to be reconstituted— counterfeit, if you will. It would be unkind to say that it tasted like a cousin of bologna, which both of my college co-ops frequently served in sandwiches, and of which I had formed a distinctly unfavorable opinion.

The best Chinese ham, *jinhua huotui,* has a texture more like

Prosciutto. Either sliced paper thin or minced, it's generally used in small quantities to enhance and invigorate a dish. In China, nobody eats a whole piece of ham; you wouldn't think of it. But America is a rich country, so rich that people can afford to serve a whole ham for a small party of five.

What impressed me most about my first piece of American ham was its softness. I found it symbolic. Americans had a soft life—they drove everywhere; their feet sank into luxurious wall-to-wall carpet when they stepped into their house; and they slept in soft beds with squishy mattresses. It seemed fitting that even their ham was soft, so soft that it didn't require much labor from their teeth.

Side dishes such as mashed potato and dinner rolls seemed keenly aware of their subsidiary roles—they required even less work from the teeth. But the dish that elevated softness to an entirely new level was peas. The peas at our chairman's that night, after having been canned and boiled, were mushy and decomposed, yellow and pitiful.

The last course was a huge piece of apple pie, containing the highest concentration of sugar of any food I'd had in my life. The extreme sweetness made me shudder, literally. At home, I was known to possess an extraordinary sweet tooth; my cousin Paul, who grew up in our house, used to comment that nothing was too sweet for my sweet tooth. He was proven wrong the first day I arrived in this country.

After the Taiwanese freighter deposited us in Portland, Oregon, several girls from our ship, including me, were invited to an American home. Upon hearing that a kindly American lady would treat us with ice cream and cake, we were all excited beyond words.

It was 1957. In Taiwan, real ice cream was only available in the most fashionable, luxurious area of Taipei in a shop called *Xiaomei* (Little Beauty). *Xiaomei* ice cream was famous. I heard plenty about it, but had never had any. In fact, by the time I arrived in the U.S., I had only had ice cream four times in my life. Twice in Shanghai, (the "Princess Snow White" vanilla ice cream bar) and twice in Taiwan, when we had "homemade" ice cream. We brought all the ingredients to a neighborhood water ice shop where they cranked it for us for a fee. We quickly brought it home, and our whole family devoured it in no time. Nobody got more than a few bites, but it was a rare, wonderful treat.

Water ice, which is shaved ice served with fresh or preserved fruits, is a very popular summer treat in Taiwan, but true ice cream was exotic and luxurious. As a result, our eyes practically bulged out of their sockets that day when we saw our American hostess serve us such incredibly generous portions.

The ice cream tasted a bit artificial, and the angel food cake was even more of a surprise—it was like a cloud. Taking a bite was like chomping into exceedingly sweet, soft, dissolvable puff. For the first time in my life, I reached the limits of my sweet tooth. Though hungry and greedy, not one of us managed to finish our plate.

Our first experience with American largesse.

I thought the ham feast that first night at the chairman's house in Iowa was a similar once-in-a-lifetime experience, but I was wrong. The following night, another equally immense ham and another bowl of yellow peas awaited us in a different dining room. For many nights, though the hostesses were of different ages, looks, and personalities, the ham and peas were exactly the same. Sam and I did our best to keep a straight face, only occasionally exchanging a surreptitious, commiserating look…

Welcome to Iowa.

§

Needless to say, in 1964, the city of Ames didn't have, and had never had, a Chinese restaurant. The closest big city, Des Moines, was thirty-five miles away. Its capitol building boasts a glistening gold dome, symbolizing the riches of the state. But Chinese restaurants? Two.

To use a Chinese expression, searching for a passable Chinese restaurant in such a locale was like *looking for fish in the trees*. Before we tried the first restaurant, we prepared ourselves psychologically and lowered our expectations drastically, but all our efforts came to naught. We walked out the door vowing never to go back. After several months, we mustered our courage and tried the second one.

Once more, never again.

Historically, Chinese American restaurants seemed to have originated from the first wave of Chinese immigrants to America in the nineteenth century, when as many as 300,000 bonded laborers were imported to build the Transcontinental Railroad. Typically, young men from Canton, a southern seacoast province, were recruited with a five-year contract. For a time, they arrived by the thousands per day, and were treated harshly and pitilessly as cheap labor, working and living under the most appalling conditions. Those who survived the five years (not many) were shipped back. A few managed to evade the authorities and remain in the country.

Many hole-in-the-wall eateries sprang up to serve fellow workers in those railroad-building days. The story goes that one night, around closing time, a bunch of famished Caucasians blundered into one particular restaurant, demanding to be fed. The Chinese man working in the kitchen scraped up what leftovers he had and stir-fried them together, calling the dish *chop-suey* ("a little bit of this and a little bit of that" in Cantonese.) The rest was history.

How did Chinese restaurant cooks in America manage to turn egg rolls, wontons, and fried rice—simple staples that had sustained our population for millennia—into something grotesque, totally unrecognizable and inedible? And more importantly, *why*? Did they themselves eat that stuff? Did they believe that was what American customers wanted? Who were the people that kept them in business? To this day, I don't know the answers.

But one thing that seems certain is that bad restaurants and ignorant customers are like the chicken and the egg—who knows which came first? We can't blame businesses for catering to popular taste for profit, but that often means lowering the quality of the product by catering to the lowest common denominator.

However, human beings are not mathematical entities, and people's taste can evolve or be elevated. During my years in this country, I learned that the American palate doesn't have to stay at the Sweet-and-Sour Pork level.

While I never flattered myself for being an excellent cook, my limited skills seemed to be more than adequate for our American friends. From not knowing how to boil water when I first came to this country to being barely able to cook for a family of four, my culinary potential quickly reached *my* Mount Everest. Out of necessity, however, I did accrue in the process—however reluctantly—some hands-on cooking experience, having learned the trick of adding some chopped scallions at the last moment and taking the pot off the stove at the right time.

When we reciprocated by inviting Sam's "ham and peas" colleagues for dinner, I served simple meat and vegetables cooked the Chinese way, and found our guests enjoyed the food. They seemed to come alive a notch or two. The atmosphere became more convivial—conversation livelier, laughter heartier, and eyes brighter. I was surprised and amused to hear that some thought that I entertained with flair, and that one of Sam's colleagues, after having dined at our house, often mused wistfully at his dinner table: "I wonder what the Lius are having tonight."

11.
You Can't Go Home Again

Thomas Wolfe's famous words are sad and true—you can't go home again. The simple fact is, nothing in life stays the same; inevitably, you and your home have both changed during the time you were away.

In 1968, while our family was busy adjusting to our life in Ames, my father decided we should come home for a visit. Sam and I packed up the kids and flew to Taipei for five weeks.

I was surprised, to say the least, to find Taipei had evolved from a sleepy town into a thriving metropolis in a mere decade. Understandably, though not as drastically, I was no longer the same, either.

During that first trip, one of my law school classmates organized a reunion in my honor—a buffet lunch in the famous Star Café in Taipei. I was taken aback that he chose a place that served Western food. Later I detected a pattern: my parents' friends wouldn't have dreamed of taking us to any place other than a Chinese restaurant, whereas people of my generation preferred the Western food that seemed to have come into vogue in Taiwan.

Our class of 1957 had 124 students, including twelve women. By the time of the reunion, most of us were married with children, but none of us attended with our spouse or children that day.

We had all grown up under the explicit Confucian rule: *no physical contact between men and women.* While at university, though we lived in the middle of the twentieth century, 2,500 years after Confucius, we behaved as if he were right there monitoring us. Throughout our four years sitting in the same classroom, we never exchanged a word with classmates of the opposite gender—not

63

even a greeting or glance.

The food that day was not memorable, but what stays in my mind is that, at the reunion, we were able to talk openly to one another for the very first time, freed by the passing of years and by the fact that we were now married with children. But we were still more than a little uneasy with one another.

We had all been law majors, but not many judges or lawyers were in our midst. When I tried to pay my bill, the organizer—a lawyer—said it was on him, that he was picking up the tab for everyone. I was shocked beyond words. Close to eighty of us were there, and Star Café was not cheap. It was so unnecessary, and how could he possibly afford it? During the gathering, sometimes I had felt as if I hadn't left at all, as if I were still one of them, but suddenly, to my utter astonishment, I blurted out in English. "No, no, no…you can't do that!"

As far as I can recall, nobody else seemed to think it was a big deal. My father was nonchalant, to say the least, when I told him about it later. "Don't worry," he said. "As a young lawyer, he might have gained some new clients by paying for that lunch." The Chinese can't bear to go Dutch, and everyone present would owe him a favor. *Still, a gathering so large…* In eleven years, without realizing it, I had already become irretrievably Americanized in some respects.

That trip was the first time Andrea and Clif, who were five and two, respectively, had been out of the country. I had assumed that, on the strength of our home environment, they were bicultural, perhaps even a bit more Chinese than American. But I was wrong. They were little Americans through and through.

In the five weeks we were in Taiwan, Andrea learned to speak Chinese fluently all right; however, she began every sentence with *dan shi* (but). Long before I was her age, I had already learned never to say "*dan shi.*" The reason was obvious—it was much too argumentative, and argumentative children were not tolerated in Chinese culture, especially not by my father.

Clif, for his part, burst into tears when he saw that milk didn't come in a carton from the refrigerator, but in powdered form to be mixed with water. He chose to forgo milk for the duration.

§

Three years later, my father was most displeased to learn that Sam had accepted an invitation to serve as a visiting professor at the University of Copenhagen without getting his permission, or at least consulting with him. Having fought in the Sino-Japanese War and had frequent run-ins with the Communists, he was a staunch anti-Communist, and he felt that Denmark was a country "in dangerous proximity to Russia." Since it was too late to stop us, he had to assert his authority by demanding that we take the long way around to visit them in Taiwan on the way to Denmark.

By then, Taiwan had grown even more prosperous. My parents' friends were very proud of the island's prosperity, and they demonstrated their pride by taking us to some of the greatest restaurants in Taipei. One extremely wealthy and prominent couple, mahjongg friends of my parents, invited us to an elaborate banquet at the best Cantonese restaurant. We had fifteen courses for the six of us, and I learned for the first time how fabulous Cantonese cuisine could be—delicate and exquisite beyond compare.

In addition to the food, what made this banquet memorable was an unexpected wrinkle that occurred the day before the event. My mother had scrutinized me and suddenly exclaimed: "Your eyebrows don't look right; one's thicker than the other!"

I had always known that my eyebrows were not up to par—they were thick and grew too closely toward the middle—but it was only one of many physical shortcomings made clear to me before or during my adolescence. Luckily, when I was in Missouri for graduate school, both of my two fellow female graduate students had plucked my eyebrows. Now one was thicker than the other? Had my friends simply gotten carried away? I had never noticed.

But no matter, Mother said so. Off she took me to her favorite beauty parlor to set my eyebrows right, in addition to getting my hair done. I was relieved that, of my many physical deficiencies, a beauty parlor visit easily remedied this one.

But why did she worry about my eyebrows? My mother, who was first in class in medical school, who for six long years during the Sino-Japanese War worked and supported three young children and saved us from extinction at the hands of the Japanese, was a brilliant and capable woman, far ahead of her time. After the war, however, my father relegated her to the role of a gracious hostess. By spending the rest of her life playing mahjongg, my father's favorite pastime since childhood, she had been reduced to a creature of her husband's habits. Worse, she had become just like their mahjongg friends, wasting her life away worrying about superficial problems, like my mismatched eyebrows.

Meanwhile, my father, of course, was as tyrannical as ever. After each trip home during the thirty years we lived on two separate continents, I gave thanks to the geographical distance between us—it afforded him less control. And I shuddered to think what kind of life I would have had if I hadn't left home.

However, my freedom and independence came with a steep price: for most of my life, I have to do without Chinese food.

12.

Old Gold Mountain, Here We Come!

When Sam was offered a one-year visiting-professor position in 1975 at the University of California at Berkeley, I was working as an editor for the dean of Graduate School of Iowa state University. My boss counseled me to stay put and let Sam go alone: "He'll be back in nine months. Your kids won't have to change schools, and you can keep your job." It made eminent sense, but for me, the lure of the reputedly excellent Chinese food on the West Coast was simply impossible to resist.

The Chinese name for San Francisco is literally *Old Gold Mountain*, which conjures up all sorts of exotic images of the American West. But when we arrived, the history and heritage of the city was not my primary concern. The first question out of my mouth was—and I'm not proud of this—"How many Chinese restaurants are here in the Bay Area?"

Our local friend was nonchalant in his reply, "Last I heard, about 3,500."

The number, so astonishing and overwhelming, simply took my breath away.

And our first visit to San Francisco's Chinatown! We were more excited than Columbus when he discovered the New World. Often a store sign or a window display would suck us like a magnet from one side of the street. Then a produce stand displaying certain fruits or vegetables we hadn't seen for a decade would seduce us to the other side. Soon we had to rush back over to see what a seafood market had to offer. We kept zigzagging...

In the end, the restaurant that we patronized most often was in Berkeley. What attracted us to The Yangtze River was their weekend breakfast—*shaobing, youtiao*, and soymilk. We usually added rice cake stir-fried with vegetable and pork, and stir-fried *youcai* (a green leafy vegetable) to round off the meal.

Shaobing, youtiao, and soymilk. When I was growing up, the threesome was the most quotidian of breakfast foods in China—like milk and cornflakes here. Perhaps I'm prejudiced, but I find the Chinese combination far more tasty and interesting.

Like pita bread, *shaobing* is baked and has a pocket. It is rectangular in shape, layered and encrusted with sesame seeds. *Youtiao*, sometimes called a Chinese cruller, is a pair of long, loosely connected pieces of dough, fried to a light golden puff more than triple its original size. It can be pulled apart vertically or simply folded in half horizontally and stuffed into the pocket of *shaobing*. Munched together, *shaobing* and *youtiao* offer a unique contrast of taste and texture. Their ingredients are the cheapest and most common staples—flour, oil, salt, yeast, sesame seeds—but making them requires a lot of elbow grease and experience.

Soymilk, of course, supplies the protein of the meal. Nowadays soymilk is available everywhere in the States, but not so in the mid-1970s. And American soymilk has been processed out of its authentic soy taste and texture. With vanilla or chocolate added to appeal to the Western palate, it tastes counterfeit to me. Chinese soymilk comes in two flavors only, savory or sweet. The former has minced dried shrimp, *zacai* (a spicy preserved vegetable), and scallions, while the latter is simply soymilk with sugar added. Both are always served piping hot.

Shaobing, youtiao, and soymilk share one important characteristic—they are horrendously labor intensive. Nobody could make them at home, not even in China, but they were readily available from many street vendors. On weekends our cook would buy them from the nearest stall, bringing a big pot to hold the hot soymilk. I took these foods for granted, not realizing one day I might live in a place where they wouldn't be available.

Nearly twenty years after I left home, at The Yangtze River, I bit into *shaobing* stuffed with *youtiao* and took a sip of scalding savory soymilk, and I was home again.

Apparently, we were not the only ones who felt that way.

The large hall was always full. Surprisingly, many diners were Caucasian, wielding chopsticks with ease. The Yangtze River was not a Cantonese restaurant, but I was more than surprised to find Cantonese families there—typically three generations occupying a large round table, enjoying *shaobing* and *youtiao* instead of their traditional Cantonese breakfast of tea with dim sum.

We had only managed to sample a dozen restaurants of the 3,500 when our year in California was over, much too soon. The night before heading back to Iowa, we had dinner at another favorite eatery. The Great Wall was a hole in the wall with a grandiose name, but the food was authentic and, most importantly, it was close to our house in Concord. A family from Taiwan owned the restaurant, with husband as chef, wife as hostess-cashier, and children as waiters. That night they gave us free desserts before we bid one another a fond farewell, as they were sorry to learn their faithful customers were leaving.

Their loss paled in comparison to ours, since we were returning to the land of no Chinese restaurants.

§

In Iowa, we were back to ordering Chinese dry goods long distance. In 1964, when we first arrived in Ames, it was a sorry place as far as availability of anything Chinese was concerned, and the situation had not improved at all twelve years later when we returned from Berkeley. Culture is notoriously slow to change—worse than a stubborn, lazy snail.

As a matter of fact, it was during my nearly two decades in Iowa that I developed a grudging respect for American mainstream culture, for its powerful control over what's available in stores, restaurants, movie theaters, and playhouses, practically every aspect of our lives. I felt hemmed in by two deplorable facts: I lived in a small town in the Midwest where everything was dictated by the mainstream, and I was not part of the mainstream.

For instance, during those years, we subscribed to *Time* magazine, which used to be a pretty decent publication—not as dumbed-down and commercial as it is today. I learned to harden my heart and skip over the *Time*'s cinema and theater pages. I couldn't bear to read the reviews, knowing films and plays interesting to me would never come to a theater near me, where there was a steady diet of *Batman*, *Star Wars*, and *Beneath the Planet of Apes*.

In supermarkets, shelf after shelf and aisle after aisle offered precious little I could use, and they seemed to tell me, *Get out! You don't belong here*. I felt squashed before setting foot in the store.

When one of the few Chinese families in town found a catalog of Chinese dry goods from San Francisco, I was thrilled. Several times a year, each participating family would laboriously compile a lengthy list, and we combined them to form one joint order.

The excitement weeks later when the shipment arrived by freight! We rushed to the railroad depot to divide the loot and exchange tips on how to preserve fresh ginger—freeze, in wine, in salt water, or buried in sand in a dark closet (I tried all four; none was satisfactory.) Our friends in New York or California would shake their heads in sympathy and disbelief, "You mean you can't even buy fresh ginger in the stores?" I learned how to freeze wonton skins so they wouldn't dry out (in plastic *and* in aluminum foil). And we bought canned goods galore: soy sauce, abalone, hoisin sauce, bean sauce, bamboo shoots, etc.

Most canned foods, as you can imagine, were poor substitutes for fresh, but it was either that or nothing. Each time I ordered canned bamboo shoots, for example, I would recall with profound sadness the days of digging fresh ones with my grandmother in our garden in Hangzhou after the Sino-Japanese War, when I was twelve.

Similarly, canned tofu was a far cry from the real thing. On one visit to Chinatown at a store display window, I had gazed longingly for so long at a large grindstone—envisioning fresh tofu and soymilk coming out of the apparatus (and conveniently forgetting the horrendous labor involved)—Sam had to drag me away.

I guess there is something about the food that you grew up with, something familiar and oddly comforting, that becomes part of who you are—a part of you that is very hard to part with.

13.

Silk-pulling Fruit and Scallion Pancakes

Glad tidings finally arrived three years after our return to Ames. A young couple from Taiwan, relatives of Sam's colleague, had arrived to open a Chinese restaurant named The House of Chen.

On opening day, for good fortune they wanted the first customer to be a *fully lucky person*—someone married, with a son and a daughter, and both parents living. It happened that I fit the criteria and was chosen.

Being of the conscientious sort, I arrived on time with my family in tow. What I didn't count on was that quite a few eager Caucasian diners were already pacing outside. When I reached the door just as it opened, several brushed me aside and got in half a step ahead of me. Having failed my mission, I could only hope whoever crossed the threshold first was also a *fully lucky person*.

Nearly everyone has the experience of recurring nightmares. Some people regularly dream of being chased by robbers or falling down a cliff. Sam's nightmare always revolved around a lecture— forgetting crucial notes or not being able to find the lecture hall. My nightmares were also consistent: being totally unprepared when guests showed up for dinner. I didn't know what to serve, and there was nothing in the refrigerator. These nightmares continued decades after I had stopped entertaining at home.

The opening day scene at the House of Chen eerily replicated my nightmare, except this time I was not the one in trouble. The situation was analogous to a vacuum seal—the moment the container is punctured, air naturally rushes in. And Ames—no, the whole state of Iowa—had been a vacuum as far as Chinese food was concerned. Now, when the residents heard this new restaurant would serve potstickers, tea-smoked duck, and many other exotic dishes, diners inundated the modest-sized establishment in minutes. The rest were forming a long line outside the door.

The owners and staff of the House of Chen didn't know whether to laugh or cry, and we didn't know whether to stay to bring good luck, or leave to alleviate the congestion. We could only try to reassure the staff with a smile and a gesture: "Take care of the other guests first, by all means."

It took a good three hours for us to be served. People were still streaming in. It was obvious the restaurant staff was thoroughly overwhelmed by the volume of enthusiastic clientele. I knew the best way I could help would be to stay out of the way. However, Andrea, a high school junior at the time, had learned to cook and clean at an early age, thanks to the ineptitude of her mother. Never having worked outside the home, she was curious and full of mettle, so after we ate, she stayed to lend a hand.

It was quite an experience. From top to bottom, everyone working at the new restaurant was a rookie. Every hour someone had to rush out to replenish supplies. The tumultuous kitchen was enough to make any brave soul cringe—the heat, the noise, the grease, the frantic pace, the confusion, the accidents, the relentless flow of orders, the desperate scramble to meet demands...and mountains of dirty dishes.

Andrea didn't return home until after two in the morning. She has been resentful ever since whenever she recalls that day: "You just drove off, leaving me washing dishes in that hell hole for ten hours!" Ay-yi-yi-yi...how could I have been so focused on supporting a Chinese restaurant that I sacrificed my own daughter?

Although I failed to be the first to step into the House of Chen on their opening day, the one who beat me to the door apparently *was* a fully lucky person. From day one, the restaurant enjoyed more business than the space or staff could handle. According to several reliable eyewitnesses, every day Mr. Chen wore a big smile all the way to the bank.

Truth be told, what kept the restaurant in booming business was more than luck, for it boasted an ambitious menu, offering popular Mandarin, Sichuan, and Cantonese dishes. Most of them had been unheard of in Iowa, like its signature dessert.

An impressive glazed fruit dish, *Basi Shuiguo* took two people working at two separate burners to make. One would fry the batter-coated chunks of apple or banana, and another stirred the sugar syrup. Timing and temperature were both extremely critical, for the fritter must be golden brown when the syrup was ready. Too hot, and the syrup would burn to a cinder; not hot enough, it wouldn't attain the desired viscosity. A waiter would bring the dessert to the table and lift a piece from the plate with a pair of chopsticks, the pulling motion spinning gossamer threads. The pieces of glazed fruit were immediately dipped in ice water to set the threads before serving. The Chinese name for the dessert literally means "silk-pulling fruit."

It was not surprising that Silk-Pulling Fruit became a favorite dessert at the House of Chen, but the Chens never expected that the humble scallion pancakes would become such a hit as well. A middle-aged bachelor friend of mine, dining alone one evening, ordered them out of curiosity, not realizing that it would be love at first bite. From then on, come dinnertime, through rain, snow, ice, or sleet, he would report to the House of Chen. This loyal fan, with his high forehead and striking winter cape, happily tucking into his scallion pancakes, became the restaurant's best living testimonial.

Ironically, what my friend found to be a sensational treat is, in China, a cheap snack that no respectable restaurant would have on the menu. Made with the simplest ingredients (flour, oil, salt, and chopped fresh scallions), it was typically cut like pizza into wedges and sold by the piece by street vendors.

During my high school years in Taiwan, when my father allowed me to stay after school to study for exams, my friends and I would buy thick and generous slices of scallion pancake to assuage our hunger at a cart parked on the other side of the school wall. Wrapped in small pieces of newspaper and handed over the wall, they were hot, crunchy, flavorful, and satisfying—the best comfort food we could afford.

In college, scallion pancakes or plain noodles flavored with sesame oil, soy sauce, and scallions were the cheapest items on the menu of student eateries, best-suited to my meager allowance.

Only years later did I learn that scallion pancakes were something we could make at home, for Sam knew how to make them from scratch. On many snowed-in Iowa weekend afternoons, he would mix the dough after lunch and leave it covered under a damp cloth to rest. When the dough was ready, we would call the kids to the kitchen to make the pancakes together. A reluctant participant at first, Clif eventually became so expert that in college he made batches from scratch all by himself. Both of my granddaughters love them so much that they have learned from Andrea to make them at home.

There are many different ways to make scallion pancakes. We always sautéed ours, and they came out multi-layered and flaky. The old man outside my high school wall leavened his with yeast and baked them. The House of Chen's scallion pancakes, like all Chinese-American restaurant ones, were deep-fried.

§

In addition to crowd-pleasers like Silk-Pulling Fruit and scallion pancakes, an important reason for the House of Chen's enduring success was they were able to keep their nose to the grindstone, providing the best food possible—no empty promises, cutting corners, or gimmicks, unlike some other Chinese restaurants.

For example, I remember once dining at a famous Peking duck restaurant in Toronto, where someone would strike a huge gong whenever a Peking duck was served. It was bad enough to have to tolerate the "KUANG..." when our duck was brought to the table. Just as I bit into my sliced duck wrapped in pancake, suddenly another ear-shattering "KUANG..." would sound from another table, and the food nearly caught in my throat. Someone at our table would just begin recounting an interesting anecdote, there it was, "KUANG..." again. The gong resounded all evening, so nerve-wracking that we lost our appetite, the thread of our conversation, and a significant portion of our hearing. We left as fast as we could, vowing never to return again.

Unfortunately, two years after the House of Chen opened, we moved to Oak Ridge, Tennessee. What a pity that we had waited fifteen long years for real Chinese fare, only to move away soon after it arrived.

A few years later, I accompanied Sam when he returned to Ames to give a series of guest lectures. Time seemed to have stood still for the House of Chen. Mr. Chen joked that the secret of his youthful appearance was getting smoked with his ducks every day.

Youthful appearances notwithstanding, Mr. Chen sold the restaurant and retired to the West Coast in the 1990s. In the twenty-odd years he was the chef and owner, the population of Ames grew only by approximately five thousand, but the number of Chinese restaurants multiplied more than ten times. Even with the new competition, House of Chen is still there today.

I'm not surprised.

14.

We Are Brothers Within the Four Seas

Natural law is such that if you gain something, you lose something else. One of the losses in our move from Iowa to Tennessee was, as far as Chinese restaurants were concerned, we were *almost* at ground zero again.

We moved because Sam needed to escape the politics that plagued the ISU physics department at the time. The availability of Chinese restaurants had not been in our considerations. Once we settled down, however, we found that Oak Ridge did have a Chinese restaurant—by the river less than a mile from our house. New China restaurant had been there for some time, enjoying a fine reputation among local diners. Our new Chinese friends told us that if we knew the owner or chef well and made "special arrangements," the restaurant was capable of producing authentic, exquisite banquets for us.

In other words, our friend implied that if we didn't fit those conditions, we shouldn't bother going. Coming from the Chinese culture, of course we understood the nuance of our friends' cautionary words, but we were too eager to try the only Chinese restaurant in town and chose to ignore them. The restaurant door was open, we rationalized, why couldn't we simply walk in and order a meal? Why wouldn't they welcome new customers?

The owner turned out to be surprisingly friendly when he spotted us. He was all smiles and chatted with us as if we were long-lost friends. In fact, he sported an enthusiasm derived from an old Chinese proverb—*we're brothers within the four seas*. He even came to our table to help us order.

However, the situation soon proved a bit awkward, for his

suggestions were not exactly dishes we cared for. After vetoing him twice, we felt obliged to say "Great!" to the suggestions that followed. Several "greats" later, the owner thoughtfully told the kitchen to make a special soup for us, a soup not on the menu, of *zhacai* (spicy preserved turnip) and shredded pork. Although it was not what we fancied either, we couldn't deny his demonstration of brotherly love.

When the food came, the warm feeling in my heart began to cool. My mother had a hometown expression to describe watery soup: "One shrimp makes a pot of soup; the shrimp is still jumping on the stove." The soup we were served certainly reminded me of that saying. In other words, the so-called soup was like hot water flavored with a bit of soy sauce, with hardly a whiff of turnip or pork in it.

The dishes the owner had strongly recommended were all below par, especially the Shrimp in Lobster Sauce, which he had insisted we try. It had ground beef in the sauce, not the traditional pork, and the beef was shockingly rancid. But in view of his warm smiles, how could we complain?

The owner's hospitality found its final expression in the bill. He insisted on giving us a ten-percent discount, emphasizing that he refused to make money off fellow Chinese. A discount may sound nice, but "not making money" was blatantly untrue. And when his wife, the cashier, found our son was a junior in high school, she remarked that they had few Chinese customers because "… Chinese parents are all pinching pennies to send their kids to Ivy League schools."

Stepping out of the restaurant, my head cooled by a stiff breeze from the river, I began to reflect on our experience. Sure, we had heard that some Chinese restaurants did not welcome Chinese diners because we were harder to please. But why put on such a song and dance to get rid of us? Whatever his motivation, the facts were clear: the owner claimed he didn't make any money from us, as if *he* was doing us a favor, while in essence, he had jammed shoddy food down our throats.

We learned our lesson and never returned. From then on, as far as we were concerned, we were once again in the land of zero Chinese restaurants.

15

Beware of that Big Iron Lid

 By now you may think that I am snobbish and Sino-centric about food, that I prefer mediocre, even bad Chinese food to any other cuisine. You would be wrong. I am, in fact, an equal opportunity diner. Simply put, I only seek a palatable meal, preferably with a small kernel of authenticity, and it doesn't have to be Chinese, exquisite, or in exclusive surroundings.

I have never eaten at a restaurant that serves caviar and don't wish to. Even if I could afford it, I would feel out of place in such an establishment and fail to enjoy the hoity-toity food. One of the most delicious meals I have eaten was at a Turkish hole-in-the-wall outside Encinitas, California, cooked by a man who could barely speak English.

In fact, my taste has always been rather pedestrian, and I prefer food honestly prepared. For this reason, I'm fascinated by so-called "street eats." I like the idea of millions of food trucks and carts hawking different foods on big city streets—the infinite varieties. Each features a few special items, distinct in their ethnicity and flavors.

My grudge against American mainstream was that it so often dictated uniformity. Just think about it. Even God didn't do that. He didn't make us from a cookie cutter; why should we eat cookie-cutter food?

When I first came to this country, restaurants were dominated by what I call the *American Culinary Trinity*. Americans were surprisingly and maddeningly conservative about food. If you drove from coast to coast and had to eat at a Howard Johnson's or a roadside diner every meal, you had three choices—steak, hamburger, or fried chicken. For me, after three days, my stomach would grow a big iron lid. No matter how hungry I was, that lid would slam shut at the thought of the trinity.

Tolstoy famously said that happy families are all alike; every unhappy family is unhappy in its own way. But I think food is just the opposite: bad meals are all alike—they are boring and inedible—while every good meal is good in its own way.

For example, several of my most memorable meals I enjoyed while traveling in South America.

In the late 1980s, when we were still living in Tennessee, Sam accepted an invitation to teach at a workshop in Brazil. It seemed like a good opportunity for me to tag along to see a bit of South America. We knew nothing about Brazilian food, and I was rather wary of that iron lid in my stomach.

The workshop was held in Brasilia, the capital, and we had our first real Brazilian meal in the nearby village of Cristalina. At lunchtime, our "tour guide," a local physics professor, took us to the best restaurant in the village.

The first thing that arrived at the table was a crudely-fashioned, much-used wooden stud, approximately five-inches square and eighteen-inches high. The top portion of the stud had several small slits cut into the wood. Professor Olivera told us those indentations were for holding the grilled meat. He ordered four varieties for our party of five—pork, lamb, chicken drumsticks, and sausage.

In the dining room heavy with the alluring aroma of barbecue, our party waited hungrily while the meats were grilled outside. Finally, we saw our waiter approach, holding high in both hands metal skewers of sizzling chunks of meat, as if they were torches. The skewers, more than three feet long with wooden handles, looked more like swords. After being inserted into the slits, they rose so high on the wood stud that we had to look up to admire them.

The meat was grilled perfectly, crisp on the outside and tender inside. Accustomed to bland American steaks and hamburgers that needed Worcestershire sauce or ketchup to jump start our taste buds, I was more than pleasantly surprised to find the Brazilian meats had been marinated in parsley, garlic, salt, and olive oil before hitting the fire.

Four dishes accompanied the meats: Brazilian rice, black beans with salted pork, French fries, and tomato slices. The steaming rice, each grain almost translucent, with a slight yellow tint and a firm texture, was surprisingly flavorful—a far cry from the bland and soggy Uncle Ben's in America. Later I learned that the rice was sautéed in lard with chopped onions and garlic before being added to the boiling water.

The black beans were coated with granules that looked like coarsely grated Parmesan cheese, but the granules had a mild, delicate flavor and were not salty like cheese. Professor Olivera told us it was cassava powder, also called manioc, a root vegetable similar to potato. It contains cyanide in lethal concentrations, and Sam had heard stories in Taiwan of boys dying from eating cassava dug from the ground and roasted. After a rigorous detoxification process, however, the cassava powder can be sautéed in oil to form golden brown granules and is such a favorite in Brazil that it's present at every meal. Cassava powder on black beans with salted pork proved to be a marvelous combination.

Even more than the delicious food, I appreciated that the meal was served family-style. It brought home to me the fact that I have always felt uncomfortable with the American way of restaurant dining. Raised knowing nothing but family style, I find the American way unfriendly, inflexible, and harsh.

Western individualism is so pervasive that it carries over to sharing a meal in a restaurant. People are seated at the same table, supposedly enjoying a time of communion, but each person orders his own dinner, thereby encountering a completely different dining experience. Sharing one another's food is deemed bad manners or crude behavior, and the edge of the plate implicitly serves as a strict boundary not to be crossed.

(*Ahhh*...speaking of boundaries, what a minefield for people from a different culture! How many times have I unwittingly overstepped the boundary with my American-born children and Americans in general, simply because in my culture, my behavior would be considered acceptable, caring, and even generous! But I digress.)

Western individualism lets you choose what you want for dinner, but it gives you only one chance—if you make the wrong choice, you are out of luck for that particular meal.

And you are limited to a set portion, determined not by you but by the restaurant, which serves the same quantity of food to every customer, whether a 280-lb football player or an eighty-pound elderly lady. If the latter is incapable of finishing her plate, she can take the leftovers home, or the busboy will cheerfully scrape it into the garbage.

For these reasons, the every-man-for-himself dining experience invariably contributes to my sense of alienation in this country. But for my first authentic Brazilian meal, I didn't have to agonize over what to order, was able to sample every dish in the amount that I desired, and enjoyed the meal thoroughly.

It also made me realize that no matter how hard I tried to adapt, how well I thought I *had* adapted, something foreign remained. Somewhere in me will always lurk the *alien*, separating and isolating me, rendering me unable to assimilate fully. After all these years, I still experience life as an outsider, looking at and reacting to what's around me from the prism of my alien sensibilities.

§

Exploring the streets of Brasilia, I saw large pieces of salted pork and huge sacks of rice, black beans, and cassava powder in the supermarkets and came to appreciate their importance in the local diet. I was surprised to learn that in the tropics, cassava is the third largest source of carbohydrates, after rice and corn. At a faculty barbecue dinner during our stay, both before and after the meal, guests were dipping their spoons into bowls of cassava powder with the same relish as Americans chomping potato chips at parties or popcorn at the movies.

Brazil is the fifth largest country in the world and by far the largest in South America, and it is rich in natural resources. The Amazon River, the most bio-diverse in the world, runs mainly within Brazil. We were told that if you consumed a different kind of fish from the Amazon every single day, you couldn't exhaust the list of varieties in a year. It was mind-boggling. And Brazilian cuisine, blending culinary traditions of India, Portugal, and Africa, is undisputedly one of the best in South America.

The best-known Brazilian dinner is *Feijoada Completa,* or Black Bean Feast. For the traditional feast, various meats (pork ears, pork tail, and sausage as well as beef tongue, salted pork, and ham hocks) are simmered for hours in one gigantic pot with black beans. When it comes time to serve, the beans stay in the pot, and the meats are cut into large thick slices, typically with beef tongue in the middle of a huge platter, salted pork and sausage at one end, fresh pork and hocks the other. A diner may ladle a portion of rice on his plate, drench it with black beans and soup from the pot, serve himself the meat slices, add sautéed shreds of collard greens, orange slices, hot sauce or whatever else is available. Lastly, the whole caboodle may be sprinkled with a thick layer of cassava powder and mixed.

With its wide array of ingredients, the *Feijoada Completa* reminded me of the Chinese *Fo Tiao Qiang,* one of the most luxurious, if not the most, of Chinese dishes.

Traditional *Fo Tiao Qiang* contains around twenty of the most prized ingredients, among them shark fin, sea cucumber, abalone, dry scallops, quail eggs, Jinhua ham, pork hocks, lamb, chicken, duck, mushrooms…You get the idea. And the preparation process is horrendously elaborate—under expert hands, it takes three days.

The name literally means "Buddha jumps over the wall." It's a legendary soup slow cooked in earthenware used to store famous Shaoxin wine. The legend goes that the aroma of *Fo Tiao Qiang* was so enticing and irresistible that if the dish were being cooked nearby, even Buddha—a staunch vegetarian—would have been tempted to jump over the wall for a taste.

The ingredients and sophistication of the Brazilian *Feijoada Completa* may not come close to the Chinese *Fo Tiao Qiang;* nevertheless, the two were born from the same idea: if one thing tastes good, a symphony of multiple good ingredients must taste that much better.

I've never had the good fortune to taste *Fo Tiao Qiang,* but I did get to enjoy *Feijoada Completa* during our stay in Brazil. I can still see those six iron pots on the long table in our hotel dining room displaying steaming hot, pitch-black soup. Floating in the soup were certain unidentifiable objects, having been rendered black by the company they kept. The Americans in our group took one look, immediately christened what was in the pots "witch's brew" and refused to try. The Brazilians, of course, couldn't wait to get their hands on it, while Sam and I were game for the experience.

The beef tongue was superb; the salted pork and ham hocks melted in our mouths, extremely salty but delicious. As instructed, we ate them with the Brazilian rice and other garnishes, and a salad of tender buds of palm leaves. They made quite a conglomerate of flavors and textures to please the palate.

Is *Feijoada Completa* on a par with *Fo Tiao Qiang*? I wouldn't think so. But thanks to it—and other Brazilian specialties—in all our two weeks in Brazil, the big iron lid in my stomach never made its appearance.

Not once.

PART III:

I Survived My Daughter's Kitchen and Other True Stories

16.

Foreigners Love Chinese Food

Having cut my teeth on Chinese food and lived my first two decades in China, I used to hold the firm conviction that Chinese food was the best in the world. By extension, I also believed that all foreigners love Chinese food. How could I not? All my compatriots felt the same way.

Of all the nationalities, we Chinese are the most chauvinistic about our food, even more than the French. And with good reason—our country boasts 5,000 years of history and culture, with our culinary art one of the most important components. Despite losing every war to Western powers in the nineteenth century, we would never concede defeat on the culinary front. It only takes one bite, we believe, for any foreigner to raise a white flag with both hands.

In my case, that belief met its first challenge during my senior year in college in Taiwan, when we invited a foreigner home for dinner.

Our guest was a former fellow student of my brother Charley, who had left home two years earlier to attend graduate school at Montana State College. Having graduated from the R.O.T.C. program there, Tim was sent to Taiwan for military service. We were told he had never had Chinese food in his life. Indeed, he looked quite excited when he arrived at our house.

My mother, naturally, was also a firm believer of *foreigners love Chinese food*. In addition, she had always been serious about authenticity. For this dinner, she planned to serve ten courses—the norm for such occasions—and took pains to ensure that each course was representative of the best that Shanghai cuisine (her specialty) had to offer.

Assigned to be the interpreter for the evening, I had looked up the English words for the dishes and their major ingredients. And I started the evening by teaching our cowboy guest, who grew up on a cattle ranch and was no doubt adept at wielding whips and lassoes, how to use chopsticks.

He didn't disappoint us. Tim's chopsticks skills were adequate in half an hour. More importantly, he seemed to be astonished and thrilled throughout the meal. Indeed, it was love at first bite with each dish. And he was delightfully curious, interested in learning about those "wondrous" dishes. While we were pleased that our mother's choice of food was so successful, we were hardly surprised. Tim simply confirmed what we had always known: *foreigners love Chinese food.*

Over the course of the dinner, however, our feelings underwent a gradual and subtle change, from delight to, shall I say, pity. We began to feel sorry for him. This guy obviously was passionate about Chinese food, yet for all his life he had had to survive on steak and potatoes, had never tasted *Shizitou* (Lion's Head) or Fish Head in a Clay Pot, never laid eyes on Phoenix-Tailed Shrimp or Stewed Sea Cucumber, never heard of Crab Eggs Noodles or Eight-Treasure Sweet-Rice Pudding. He didn't even know shiitake mushrooms or dried shrimp existed. Clearly, Tim had lived his entire life in vain.

He thought every dish brought to the table was the main course, and simply couldn't fathom why one main course arrived after another, and another, and yet another. His eyes, clear blue and innocent, were brimming with questions. Finally, unable to contain himself any longer, he inquired, "Do you eat like this every night?"

"As a matter of fact, no," I admitted. "This dinner is more elaborate because we are having a guest. Normally we only have four dishes and a soup."

"What do you typically eat for dinner?" he persisted.

Chinese food has so many varieties. Even the lowly wood ear mushroom can be black wood ear, white wood ear, cloud ear, ground ear—about fifteen different kinds. How could I describe one typical dinner? There is no typical dinner. Besides, I had only prepared enough English to answer the most basic questions for this meal.

Suddenly I thought about the fermented tofu we had that morning. Ordinary everyday food and very different from dishes in this meal, fermented tofu is normally served at breakfast with plain porridge. It generally comes in one-inch squares in its brine, grayish in color, with a Brie-like texture.

Out of consideration for his inexperience, we served our guest the regular kind, rather than the spicy. When it was brought to the table, given his curiosity, youthful exuberance, and the confidence he'd gained from the previous dishes, he took a big bite before I had a chance to coach him.

He didn't do well. In fact, he was in shock, and his shock quickly turned to pain. Facing a table full of people watching him expectantly, he struggled to find some tactful words and came out with:

"Salty, isn't it?"

§

Fermented tofu is a drop in the bucket as far as Chinese food is concerned, and—again, like Brie—it's an acquired taste. If Tim had begun judiciously with a tiny morsel, he might have found it rather delightful and interesting. Unfortunately, I had not been savvy enough to prepare him. I was sorry that he had such a shock, but the incident only slightly dented my belief that *foreigners love Chinese food*.

It was only after I came to this country that my conviction was truly challenged. During my second year at the University of Missouri, in 1960, came the exciting news in our small circle of Chinese students that my former roommate Pearl had just married her Caucasian American classmate. It was the only mixed marriage we knew. Since Missouri law forbade interracial unions and no one in the state would perform the ceremony, they had driven to the neighboring state of Iowa to tie the knot.

I've always been impressed by American wedding vows, which seem to cover all the pitfalls that can possibly trip up a marriage— for better, for worse; for richer, for poorer; in sickness and in health. But wouldn't you know it? They neglect to include one line, especially crucial in a mixed marriage: I promise to eat whatever you eat.

Pearl's husband came from Louisiana, the conservative South. A shy, bookish young man, he was in all likelihood good at judging a book by its cover. Unbeknownst to us, he was apparently also in the habit of judging food by its cover.

After Pearl and Jim came back from their Iowa wedding and settled down, they invited us to their home for dinner—for dumplings, to be exact.

Called *jiaozi* in Chinese, dumplings are very popular from one end of China to the other. They typically contain a filling of chopped vegetables mixed with ground pork, and are served with different sauces. Since they have to be made one by one, it usually takes a group to pitch in and make a decent size batch for a meal. One person is usually in charge of rolling the dough by hand into thin, small, round pieces. The others place some filling in the middle of each piece, fold it to half-moon shape, and seal by pinching the edges together. It's like making so many tiny half pies.

That evening, while the rest of us were having a great time talking, laughing, and wrapping *jiaozi*, Pearl was busy rolling two large, round pieces of dough, stirring chopped onions, ketchup, and black pepper with ground beef, and making two extra large, fat half moons. Instead of *jiaozi*, she was making Chinese *hezi*, albeit with American filling. (Traditional Chinese *hezi* contain Chinese chives, scrambled eggs, mung bean noodles, and tiny dried shrimp.) She slid them into the oven instead of sautéing them in a skillet the Chinese way.

While the dumplings were boiling and the two large *hezi* were baked to an enticing golden hue, our hostess sweetly called to her new husband, "Jim, dear, your turnovers are ready!" So Jim sat down with us and enjoyed his *turnovers*, while Pearl and the rest of us ate *jiaozi*. Everyone was happy.

Thanks to Pearl, I gained a valuable insight that night.

A turnover is an American dessert with fruit filling inside flaky, leavened puff pastry—quite different from what Pearl made for Jim. But the latter had the same shape and were also baked. Calling them *turnovers* added legitimacy and rendered them eminently acceptable to Jim. I was greatly impressed by Pearl's ingenious way of modifying a traditional recipe and sidestepping a potentially contentious issue.

At the same time, I thought of our erstwhile cowboy guest. The poor chap deserved a lot of credit for trying, in one dinner, so many new foods for the very first time. We had chosen each dish with good intention, without realizing how difficult it might be for him. We were chauvinistic and unwittingly cruel; it took the fermented tofu to bring the truth home to us.

Pearl and I lost touch for some forty years. In those four decades, Jim—James Lee Burke—became a bestselling author of more than thirty mystery and crime novels. We reconnected when he and Pearl were in San Diego for a book tour. I asked Pearl whether Jim still refused to eat *jiaozi*. She laughed, "He eats everything now, and he really likes *jiaozi*." No more beef *turnovers* for Jim.

§

During my last summer in Missouri, when almost all the Chinese students departed in pursuit of summer jobs, I stayed on at Rochdale House to finish my thesis. The house was largely empty, and we remaining girls were fending for ourselves for meals. Fortunately, my friend Patricia Chang, a young University librarian still in town, was kind enough to invite me often to her apartment for dinner.

I longed to reciprocate Pat's hospitality, but was hampered by the fact that I didn't know how to cook, and had no desire to learn. I can't recall what I did in those days to feed myself, but I remember vividly the more starved I was, the more I craved something I could not have and would never eat again: *cairoubao*, the vegetable and meat buns from *Yinyi*, Taipei's best restaurant specializing in the food of my father's region, Huaiyang.

I never had the fortune to set foot in *Yinyi*, but I had dearly loved their *cairoubao*. Occasionally, our maid was sent to buy the buns when the cook was too busy to make afternoon snacks for our mahjongg guests.

And how exquisite they were! You could see the emerald green of the coarsely chopped vegetables through the dough. The filling, mixed with pork, was tender, moist, translucent and still tasted like fresh Shanghai bok choy with a touch of natural sweetness. One heavenly bite spoiled my appetite for regular meat buns for the rest of my life—the dough is invariably too thick and the fillings are tough and dry, as if made of horse meat. (Admittedly, I've never had horsemeat, but I can imagine what it's like.)

To make any kind of meat buns, you have to start with leavened dough, and I knew enough not to attempt the impossible. One day, however, I had the inspiration of using Pillsbury biscuit dough instead. I could put in some filling, steam them, and invite Pat to share the meal! They wouldn't hold a candle to *Yinyi*'s *cairoubao*, but they'd be better than nothing.

When the steamed buns were ready and I opened the lid of the pot, two housemates at the kitchen table, gnawing on their bologna sandwiches, exclaimed, "What smells so wonderful?"

Forgetting the *turnover* lesson and perceiving a great opportunity to introduce these girls to Chinese food, I invited them to eat with us. When they saw what was on the plate, the two, who had been so sorely tempted by the aroma, shook their heads in disappointment, "The bread is still white. It's raw!"

I should've explained they were not baked and therefore couldn't be brown, but I didn't think of it. Instead, I opened one to prove they were not actually bread and shouldn't be judged by the same standards. It was a mistake. They saw that there was filling inside, the filling was not fruit but ground meat, and worst of all, the meat was not beef but pork. "Your filling is also raw! Raw pork has parasites. Unless you heat it to 185 degrees, you'll get trichinosis!"

Deflated but still hopeful, I was ready to argue my case. "What make you think the pork's raw?"

"The color! It's still pink!"

I lost my patience. Signaling Pat with my eyes, I carried the buns to the dining room. "We're going to enjoy them. I have eaten what you call raw pork for more than twenty years, and I don't have trichinosis."

They followed us to the dining room, pleading all the while, "Please, for heaven's sake, don't eat them! Trichinosis is asymptomatic. You wouldn't want parasites in your muscles."

By the time I got rid of the two biology majors, the buns were cold. Their aroma had dissipated and they tasted flat. Patricia looked preoccupied; she didn't seem to have an appetite, while I thought I saw something lurking in the filling. We were both spooked, and ate the buns cautiously.

§

That experience effectively killed my belief that *foreigners love Chinese food*. In later years, however, I gradually found Americans' acceptance of Chinese food was often nuanced, with myriad forms and levels.

Take the neighbor across the street from us in Ames, a professor of agriculture. He was a very principled person—his principle being his mouth was not made to chew meat and vegetables simultaneously. Confucius had stipulated *no physical contact across the gender line*. For this man, there couldn't be physical contact between meat and vegetables. He simply would not tolerate most Chinese dishes: forget beef hanging out with broccoli, or peas getting mixed up with chicken, not to mention any other promiscuous or unmentionable characters such as bean curd and bamboo shoots.

While I admired his principle, I was sorry that he could not carry it to its logical conclusion. He needed two digestive systems, one for meat and another for vegetables.

Then there was the wife of Sam's colleague who refused to eat duck, her reason being "I've never had duck in my life." I could only be happy that she didn't insist on this principle from day one. Otherwise she would have starved to death after refusing milk for the same reason, and would not have survived to reject duck.

Compared with these two timid eaters, Americans who love egg rolls, fried rice, and Moo Goo Gai Pan are truly brave souls. They have taken the risk—a quantum leap toward the unknown. It's a shame that most of them remain so loyal to this standard Chinese American restaurant fare that they never stray.

In general, most Americans brought up with hamburgers and french fries harbor various degrees of reservation about Chinese food, however much they may think they love it. Their reservation in turn feeds the Chinese assumption that Americans can't accept real Chinese dishes. When an occasional adventuresome

American wishes to try something out of the ordinary at a Chinese restaurant, he is likely to be discouraged by the waiter—"Forget it. You're not going to like it."

And then there are other foreigners who use chopsticks as if they were born with them. They are at home with Sichuan food, the spicier the better. They can cite dishes many Chinese don't even know, and they don't flinch at the sight of a whole fish, complete with head and staring eyes, or a Cantonese roasted duck with head, neck, and claws.

At a conference in Philadelphia many years ago, Sam went to dinner in Chinatown with two Caucasian physicists from New York who loved Chinese food. The three of them ordered four dishes, including a steamed whole fish.

Sam loved fish, especially the head. He often claimed that he had been a cat in his last reincarnation. That evening the fish had an unusually nice, big head. The waiter, consciously or not, put the fish right in front of Sam, who figured he was in no hurry to eat the head, as he would have no competition.

Before he finished thinking, the two pairs of chopsticks of his colleagues were already going for the you-know-what. The one across from him got there first. He gave his chopsticks a practiced twist and popped the fish head into his bowl, leaving Sam with his jaw open. Because of his prejudice that *foreigners don't eat fish heads*, Sam had lost his chance. Sam never underestimated *foreigners* in that regard again.

17.
The Sesame Oil Incident

Shortly after Sam and I married and moved to Mount Kisco, New York, we met two other young couples in our apartment complex. They were very friendly, and the wives often expressed interest in Chinese food, to the point I felt obliged to invite them for dinner. I had not cooked for *foreigners* since the disastrous Rock 'n' Roll Eggs experience. Naturally, I gave the menu a lot of thought.

Back in Taiwan, I had attended mandatory sessions given by the Ministry of Education in which we were exhorted to engage in citizen diplomacy and be cultural ambassadors. I was determined to do my best to carry out my diplomatic mission, and this dinner seemed a golden opportunity.

Of course I wasn't going to serve the clichéd Sweet and Sour Pork. As a matter of fact, I didn't have the foggiest idea how to make Sweet and Sour Pork. I decided to make my easier, adapted version of Charley's egg dumplings.

After making more than six of my large egg rolls, I still had a few egg crepes but had run out of filling. Toss them in the garbage like that shockingly profligate Mrs. Smithson, for whom I had made the Rock 'n' Roll Eggs years before? Not on your life! Having grown up in wartime, I am pathologically incapable of throwing away food.

To use modern lingo, I tried to think outside of the box. I cut the egg crepes into long, thin, noodle-like strips, added shredded cucumbers and cooked ham, and tossed my tri-color "masterpiece" with typical Chinese condiments before serving it as a side dish that evening.

Our guests obviously had never encountered improvised Chinese dishes like mine, and they seemed pleasantly surprised. They ate heartily and praised my food so extravagantly that I was on cloud nine.

One of the ladies, Jenny, seemed especially impressed. "Everything's so delicious, and your cucumber salad is just out of this world! What's the secret of your wonderful dressing?"

I told her I used sesame oil, not regular salad oil. In 1961 it would have been rare to find a Caucasian American who had heard of sesame oil. When Jenny seemed puzzled, I added, "We always use sesame oil to season our cold dishes, for its great flavor."

"Sesame oil? How interesting! May I taste a drop?" asked Jenny's husband Eddie.

"Of course!" Encouraged by their interest, I went into the kitchen and brought out a small bottle.

"Why is it so dark?" Eddie was an engineer, observant and in the habit of getting to the bottom of things. He was right. The various oils sold at supermarkets were light in color, not dark brown like sesame oil.

"We buy our sesame oil from Chinatown, made in Taiwan from roasted sesame seeds—a Chinese method," Sam was happy to explain. "The Japanese also love sesame oil, but they use raw seeds. Their oil is light in color and not very flavorful." (Years later, however, the Japanese also started to use roasted seeds.)

Sam was so proud of his knowledge that I feared he was going to launch into an impromptu lecture on the subject. Luckily, he checked himself.

Our guests took turns pouring a little oil on the plate and tasting it tentatively with the tip of their fork. Full of smiles and genuinely pleased, they were unanimous: "It's marvelous!"

But I noticed all four stopped eating the salad, leaving what was already there on their plates. I understood enough about Western etiquette at that time to know that leaving all that food untouched showed that something was seriously wrong. Contrary to what people think about the polite, inscrutable Orientals, under the same circumstances, our Chinese friends wouldn't have kept silent.

When Jenny helped me take the plates to the kitchen, I asked her in a low voice, cutting to the chase, "Didn't all of you say that you loved the salad? Why did everybody stop eating it?"

She was taken aback. She hesitated and turned to me apologetically, "I don't know about the others, but I felt that sesame oil—I'm terribly sorry—tastes a bit like...eh...*burned hair*. I hope you don't mind, do you?"

Do I mind? What choice do I have in a sea of people bent on emphasizing only the positive, to the point of ignoring, denying the truth? Garrison Keillor is only half kidding when he says all the children in Lake Wobegon are above average.

It intrigued me that the previously "delicious" salad dressing suddenly turned "burned hair" when they found it contained sesame oil, an unfamiliar, *foreign* ingredient. Being American and behaving like well-meaning guests at dinner, they felt obliged to uphold a positive façade as if everything had been hunky dory.

In time, I did learn not to raise a mental eyebrow at this bizarre cultural tendency. Nevertheless, after all my years here, I still prefer to call a spade a spade, even if I can't always do so openly in this culture.

18.

Friendship and Meatballs

Penny was one of my roommates and my best friend at Rebec House in Oregon. She had to be. *A friend in need is a friend indeed.* Penny and I were truly friends in need—especially every other Thursday evening and every Saturday night.

While the dozen Chinese students at the University of Oregon had been unanimously opposed to my moving into an American (!) women's cooperative house, I had my own considerations. True, it was the cheapest university housing, but it was still more expensive than the room I was renting in a house next door—financially, I'd have been better off staying put. But I had two problems: I'd grown increasingly fearful of the burly landlord who hugged me every time he came to my room to collect the weekly rent, *and* I didn't know how to cook. I needed safer accommodations with meals included.

After moving into Rebec House, however, I realized I had a different price to pay. Our president told me that the essence of a cooperative house is the spirit of cooperation. We shared all the work and participated in all the social activities. No exceptions.

One important social activity turned out to be the "exchange" candlelight dinner every other Thursday, when we sent half of our members to a men's co-op, and they dispatched half of theirs to us. We had to dress up for it, the men in suits and ties and women in our nice dresses.

And that was not all. A dance was always held after dinner, and for two long hours of the dance, Penny and I were always the wallflowers.

America in the 1950s was not the diverse society of today. Few

American male college students in that day had ever laid eyes on an *Oriental* female, and not surprisingly, they stayed away from me. Though Penny was Caucasian, her unpopularity had everything to do with her height and appearance. She was large-boned and tall, six-feet tall. I had never seen a girl this tall in my life. She'd be great shooting a basketball, but as a dance partner she was downright unapproachable. And she had a long face, with acne scars plainly visible even in candlelight.

Everyone says *beauty is only skin deep*, but don't you believe it! The fact is, that skin-deep beauty determines your life. Penny seemed to have suffered a great deal of rejection from the opposite sex growing up, and by college age she was resigned and cynical, and had totally abandoned the possibility of being attractive to men.

Therefore, at the dances when the number of women outweighed the men, which was most of the time, Penny and I always sat in a corner, trying to while away the excruciating hours by pretending to chat with each other.

On the surface, Rebec members, despite coming from families less affluent than those of the sorority and dormitory girls, seemed to me to be the luckiest people in the world—they certainly didn't have any of the problems I had. But by and by, I found those lucky girls had their troubles, too. It was perfectly fine to flunk a midterm, or receive the lowest grade on a paper, but not having a date on Saturday night was the most humiliating and shameful thing on Earth.

Under this pressure, every girl tried her utmost to snatch a boyfriend. Once you secured one, you were all set—no more worries about weekend dates. Those who didn't have a boyfriend would scour their social worlds to land a blind date. Staying home was unthinkable.

I was going steady, too—with the University library. The trouble with having the library as a *boyfriend* was that he didn't care a whit about me. Every night promptly at ten o'clock, he would kick me out, no matter how desperately I wished to linger. Worst of all, on the all-important Saturday nights he even refused to open his door.

Hence on Saturday nights, Penny and I would be left alone in the eerily quiet Victorian, three-story house. I would have loved to use the precious hours to catch up on my schoolwork, but soon was made to understand that it was sacrilegious to study on a Saturday night. So Penny and I would talk until midnight, waiting for all the girls to return radiant at curfew hour, laughing and shouting about what a great time they had had. (It was unforgivable to not have had a fabulous time on a date.)

Despite her looks, Penny was no shrinking violet. She had a strong personality, was rather opinionated, and enjoyed teaching this foreigner a thing or two. Though I had no trouble distinguishing "rice" from "lice," I only learned to differentiate "towel" from "tower" after her repeated corrections.

However, sometimes she pushed her advantages too far. For instance, I used Saturday nights to do my week's laundry, and Penny would often comment, "You're going to miss our washing machine when you go home. It'll be so much work to wash everything by hand!"

What she said and the way she said it rubbed me the wrong way. I had to strike back: "No, we have a better washing machine: I drop my clothes on the floor, and the next time I see them, they're in my drawer—washed, ironed, and folded."

She was speechless. She couldn't imagine my having a maid at home to do the housework any more than I could have anticipated everyday American life before I arrived. We were both young and ignorant, and we came from entirely different cultures; we didn't really understand—or have the maturity to try to understand—each other.

Although Penny and I had our occasional spats, the fact we had been friends in need meant something to both of us. After nine months, I left Oregon and gradually lost touch with everyone—except Penny. She went to Kansas City and married an engineer from Pakistan. One year, when her husband went home to see his family, she decided to drive to New York and visit me. By that time I was married, expecting my first child.

Strangely, seeing Penny again after four years was almost like reuniting with a family member. She seemed to feel likewise, and believe she had the seniority—after all, she had met me long before Sam did. She thought Sam was "very nice, but too skinny," and she was determined to use her weeklong visit to help him gain some much-needed weight.

Most Americans would not consider the weight of a friend's husband any of their business. But on this issue, Penny was obviously a notable exception. In fact, she was acting very much like a Chinese—taking on a friend's *problems* as if they were her own. The fact I was a foreigner and a whole foot shorter probably also triggered her altruistic instinct. In any case, she voiced the opinion that Sam's breakfast—a boiled egg, a piece of toast, and a glass of orange juice—was inadequate. Why not double everything and switch the boiled egg to butter-fried eggs?

While flattered that my friend took such interest in his welfare, Sam was worried. "I don't think I can eat all that food."

With an authoritative wave of her hand, Penny answered, "You'll get used to it."

Sam's performance the next morning exceeded everyone's expectations—he cleaned up his double portion in a matter of minutes. Penny nodded to me, smiling, "You see?"

Next, she felt Chinese meals, though tasty, were not as nutritious and calorie-dense as good old hearty American fare. The third day after her arrival, after touring the Empire State Building, she asked me to take her food shopping, so that she could cook us a decent dinner. She would be the chef, and I, her assistant.

Penny proved to be a great cook and we raved about the meal. Her spaghetti and meatballs was extraordinary delicious, the sauce rich and aromatic, and the pasta delightfully al dente. Sam was first to finish his plate, and Penny, serving spoon ready, persuaded him to have a second helping.

Persuade, of course, is an understatement. Before Sam had swallowed the last bite of the first mountainous serving, Penny was already raising the large ladle for seconds.

He shook his head, "Please, no, I really can't eat anymore. I already had more than I should because it was so delicious."

"Of course you can! Didn't you eat up your breakfast when you thought you couldn't?" She filled his plate again.

Sam sighed. *Your guest drove halfway across the country and cooked a wonderful dinner for you. How could you let her down?* The second mountain also started to disappear, albeit at a much slower pace. Our chef's smile was getting broader and deeper. She and I were chatting when suddenly Sam shot up from the table with a hand on his mouth. The noise he made in the bathroom was unmistakable— the dinner Penny labored over was going, going, gone!

What followed was like a film in fast forward. Penny's face changed. She got up and announced that she was going for a walk. It was already completely dark outside, but I couldn't dissuade her. She was gone for almost an hour, and the doorbell didn't ring until I had already cleaned up the kitchen.

Standing outside the door, Penny announced that she had decided to drive back to Kansas City that night. I tried, in vain, to talk her into at least waiting till the next morning. Helplessly watching her throw her clothes into her suitcase and drive off in a huff, I felt my heart as heavy as my spaghetti-laden stomach.

Next morning, Sam went back to his single portion breakfast.

And I had time to mull over the word *friendship*, which seems to imply people on the same ship sharing both fortunes and misfortunes. But the famous American satirist Ambrose Bierce had a different take. In *The Unabridged Devil's Dictionary*, Bierce defines friendship as "a ship big enough for two in fair weather, but only one in foul." In other words, friendship rarely survives the test of a big storm.

Bierce was cynical, but there is some truth in his words. The meatballs in that spaghetti were not meatballs, they were torpedoes that blew several large holes in our friendship. We didn't know how to save it, and could only stand by and watch it sink to the bottom of the sea.

After Penny went home, our correspondence became sporadic. A year or so later, I received a Christmas card with a few words informing us she had a son and was recently divorced. After that, the cards I sent hit a dead end. She was completely out of touch.

Interestingly, however, Old Man Time accomplished quite effortlessly what Penny had worked so hard to achieve. Before I knew it, my scrawny husband went from a lightweight to middleweight without eating one extra egg or one additional serving of spaghetti.

By then—what a shame—Penny was long gone from our lives and we had no way of telling her the good news.

19.
Hospitality, American style

It's ironic that the great American genius Thomas Edison invented the electric light and the phonograph, thus contributing significantly, albeit indirectly, to the popularity of an American social institution he loathed—the cocktail party.

As the story goes, the hearing-impaired luminary once was persuaded by his wife to attend a party, and was surrounded by admirers upon arrival. He finally managed to retreat to a corner far from the madding crowd, where a friend edged near him unnoticed and heard him sigh, "If there were only a dog here!"

I must admit I was incredulous when I first read this story. Growing up in Taiwan, I had watched parties in American movies in awe and with envy, where elegant ladies and gentlemen exchanged clever repartee, waving their long-stemmed glasses. It was glamorous, stimulating. Why did Edison detest it so?

Little did I know that after numerous parties, mostly in the latter half of the 1960s in Ames, Iowa, I would come to empathize with him on this very subject.

During Edison's time, the cocktail party belonged to high society. However, in this democratic country, the trend soon spread to the middle class, to the point where many of us had the opportunity to attend such wondrous festivities.

The cocktail party is indeed the most efficient and economical way of discharging one's social obligations. And it's so very American. It does not require elaborate cooking. Interaction with the guests is minimal, so one is spared the hassle of communicating with them or getting to know them. Cleaning the house is unnecessary, since wall-to-wall people will conveniently obscure any stains on the wallpaper or dust balls in the corners.

I suspect, to compile a guest list for a cocktail party, the rule of thumb was one warm body per square foot plus thirty percent. The rationale may have been that some guests would arrive late and others leave early. During the peak hours, if the weather permitted, guests could always spread to the deck and the backyard.

On the night of the party, those of us honored with an invitation would arrive dressed up in our party clothes. Cars were parked bumper-to-bumper for blocks. The house, aglow inside and out and more crowded than Grand Central Station at rush hour, would literally burst at its seams—the combined din of voices, laughter, and music seeping from the structure like steam from a pressure cooker on a red-hot stove.

It does take a great deal of courage to walk into a gathering of such magnitude. I don't mean to pat myself on the back, but generally, all I needed was to grit my teeth and steel my nerves, and I was ready. As seasoned party attendees, Sam and I wouldn't ring the doorbell; we'd open the door (never locked on these occasions) and plunge right in. For the motto of the evening was *help yourself.* If we should manage a rare sighting of the host or the hostess, all they would say to us was "Help yourself."

Once inside, we'd fight the crowd into the master bedroom, leaving coats, gloves, scarves, and purse on the bed (already piled high) and make our way in the direction of the food and the booze.

This was easier said than done. In reality, the closer we were to the refreshments, the higher the population density, and the better the probability of being waylaid by someone. On one occasion when I failed to reach the victuals all evening, I began to respect the wisdom once imparted by a friend: "Always try to invite a lot of people, because the more people, the less each will consume."

By now I had usually lost sight of Sam. It was every man for himself.

When I reached my destination, I had a different problem. I am allergic to alcohol, and neither caffeine nor sugar likes me, so I could only drink water. Before the age of Perrier and later, the advent of bottled water, I would usually have to turn around and somehow navigate my way to the kitchen tap.

Attacking the assorted edibles presented a different challenge. Over the years, I learned to slice meat or cheese with my right hand, while clutching napkin and paper plate with my left pinky and ring finger, and balancing a paper cup with my left thumb and index finger. The cup and plate might shake and dance, but I hold the world record for never having lost a morsel of food or spilled a drop of water.

Refreshments in hand, it was time to fulfill my duty as a party guest and circulate. In this egalitarian society, everyone simply must have a marvelous time. Standing shoulder-to-shoulder, perched in front of the piano, or wedged between the refrigerator and the kitchen counter, everyone indeed looked radiant and happy, talking and laughing with expansive gestures and great animation. Silence certainly was not golden here. It was time to gather my might, pit my vocal chords against hundreds of others and the booming stereo, and scream into my nearest neighbor's ear with a smile: "HOW ARE YOU? I'M FINE!"

Here I must confess my handicap. At five-foot-two in my prime, I had to wear three-inch heels in order to huddle with fellow guests a few inches taller. For six-footers, even my heels were no help. I had to stand on tiptoe, crane my neck, and wait for him to bend over before we could yell hello. Obviously, neither of us could sustain such postures for long, so we soon parted ways.

In addition to the height problem, I was especially wary of two types of fellow guests—the silent one and the excessively talkative one.

Since the former didn't say much, I had to make a conscientious effort to fill the gaps. After I had said everything I shouldn't, and couldn't think of anything appropriate to say, I would let the matter run its course. A few minutes of silence, accompanied by our staring mournfully at each other, eyeball to eyeball, were enough. My companion would turn abruptly and disappear, mercifully not to be seen again for the rest of the evening.

The talkative one, on the other hand, might grab onto an exasperating topic and never let go. This usually happened with someone I hadn't met before. The stranger would start making comments such as "I just adore Moo Shu Pork," "The Chinese are a wonderful people; you are all so sweet," or "I don't understand how you Chinese stay so slim."

I would wave my half crumpled paper cup and declare, "Excuse me. I need a refill," and make my getaway. Or I'd suggest, "The cauliflower is delicious. I highly recommend it...Oh, you're not hungry? I'd better get some myself." Or I could grab someone— "Have you met Sharon?"— and while they exchanged pleasantries, I'd make my escape.

One-on-one interactions were a hard way to survive the hours at a cocktail party. An easier way was to join a group and let someone else do the talking. Nodding and smiling at appropriate moments, I could relax and let my mind wander and my vocal chords enjoy a much-deserved rest.

There was, of course, much more to a party; a party is a society in miniature. If so inclined, one might take advantage of the opportunity to cut deals, collect information, talk business, exchange ideas, cement relationships, scrutinize friends and foes, foster or mend connections, and—last but not least—flirt.

American men in those days were an interesting species. If I may generalize, many seemed to be uncomfortable with women, so they either stayed away altogether or flirted shamelessly. The cocktail party served, as I'm sure it still does today, as an adult playground. After a few drinks, Mike's wife and Stan, each wearing one of her earrings, would start slow dancing. Jimmy's significant other would be giggling on Danny's lap. Tom's girlfriend and Jerry would be sharing a cigarette and gazing deeply into each other's eyes...

By the early morning hours when the crowd began to thin, and the host and hostess appeared as if by magic, my feet were sore, my legs were numb, my vocal chords and adrenaline had both given out, and the veins in my temples were pulsating with the bass from the stereo. My paper cup had been reduced to shreds, while Sam could be found leaning exhausted against the kitchen wall. It was time to make our exit.

It was time to go home to rest up for the next party.

20.

One and a Half Cups of Coffee

W hile it may be difficult for an immigrant to adapt to many aspects of his new culture, he is nevertheless capable of falling headlong, irretrievably in love with something in his adopted country.

Like Sam with his coffee.

All his life, Sam hated shopping—he would literally age ten years simply by stepping into a store, his eyebrows and shoulders tragically sagging. But coffee stores were the exception, with those gleaming, dark brown coffee beans, nearly weightless on your palm, in wooden barrels under transparent plastic lids, with seductive names such as Mocha Java, Espresso, and Vienna Roast.

When we first arrived in the small town of Ames, it contained practically nothing except a university. Downtown consisted of a short street with a handful of stores. And it was hardly culturally diverse. People often wanted to know what brought us there, asking, "Are you students? Where are you from?"

By and by, they stopped asking. With more Asians—called Orientals at that time—as well as other ethnicities joining the university, the homogeneous town gradually acquired an ever so slight cosmopolitan air.

Downtown also expanded. One day, in an import store at our new shopping center we were thrilled to find several wooden barrels with coffee beans. However, despite the growing appreciation for food and culture, there must not have been enough locals who shared our enthusiasm because the beans were never very good— they seemed to have lost their flavor from sitting in the barrels too long. From then on Sam had a new mission: every time he attended a conference or gave a talk, whether in Europe, New York, or San Francisco, he would search for a specialty coffee purveyor.

In each shop, the strong aroma of coffee would greet him when he pushed open the door. Half inebriated from a cappuccino, which he took pains to savor fully, he would select his beans with great care and walk out with several small paper bags in hand. Despite the tight seal on the plastic-lined bags, the perfume of coffee would permeate every item in his suitcase by the time he arrived home.

Coffee became a sort of ritual—both in the making and the drinking. The Chinese don't usually drink beverages during a meal, except the occasional liquor, so it was after breakfast on weekends that Sam would begin his happiest and most relaxing hour with coffee. He loved mixing different types of beans to strive for distinct flavors. Removing several small bags from a metal canister and picking out, say, thirty French Roast beans and ten Javas, he would start grinding.

His black wrought-iron grinder sat atop a square box, and inside the box was a small drawer. Sam loved turning the grinder wheel, inhaling the coffee aroma, and watching beans disappear one by one. When he opened the drawer, the finely ground powder would be lying in a ring in the middle of the drawer.

Somehow the way Sam ground his coffee reminded me of the old man I used to watch as a child at the market in Hangzhou. My family lived in that city, known for its beautiful West Lake, after the eight-year Sino-Japanese War and before the Civil War reached us. During those preciously rare, peaceful few years, occasionally I was allowed to accompany our trusted maid to the market, where I watched with fascination an old man doing calligraphy. Before the Chinese New Year, he enjoyed a brisk business of writing celebratory couplets on long strips of red paper to be pasted on both sides of people's front doors. Other days, he would pen letters for customers. In that dingy, smelly, rowdy, and teeming market, there was something about him that struck me and stayed with me.

In my memory, the old man wrote the couplets with a gigantic brush, which he dipped in his inkwell from time to time. The inkwell and his rectangular ink stick, which he ground to make ink, were also huge, the latter with a ferocious dragon carved on one side and four words in gold—*Huang Shan son yan* (pine mist on the Yellow Mountain)—on the other side.

I was about eleven years old. My hands would have been too small to go around the ink stick, had I ever been bold enough to come close to his table to touch it. With his left hand, the old man held back the sleeve of his long gown, his right hand steadily and slowly guiding the stick in the inkwell in circles again and again…with a sort of quiet religious reverence, as if in a trance. Time stood still, the din of the market seemed to recede, and I held my breath…

§

Tenderly, Sam would pour boiling water over the coffee powder resting in a small white porcelain funnel, alternating two cups under the funnel, while coffee dripped a few drops at a time. He knew good coffee was worth the wait; it shouldn't be rushed.

When he placed the two cups of steaming coffee on the table, he was very pleased with himself, as if he had just finished a masterpiece. A half-filled cup for me, the whole cup for himself.

Caffeine was always too strong a stimulant for me; my cheeks would burn as if I were drunk, and a full cup in the morning affected my sleep at night. But it tasted too good to give up, so I compromised by occasionally drinking half a cup.

Having no way of knowing whether I could join him any given morning and nevertheless wishing for companionship, he took to waving an empty cup in front of me, "You're *not* going to have coffee today, I presume?"

If I countered, "Who says?" he would happily fetch another cup.

Every weekend for years we repeated the same dialogue, like children playing a game, until our hair turned gray.

Holding my cup with both hands, I would sometimes look out to the backyard. The slip of maple we had planted years ago now towered over our two-story house, and my memories around coffee were rendered all the more languid by the moment of quiet contemplation.

My mother liked to tell the story of our leaving Shanghai in

1937 by steamship to reunite with our father in Guizhou, where he had gone two years previously to work for the government. It was the beginning of China's eight-year war with the invading Japanese, and Shanghai had just been lost to the enemy after more than three months of bloody battles, with casualties numbering nearly 300,000. Two years old, innocent of all the bloodshed and seeing the famous waterfront for the first time, I was beside myself with excitement and exclaimed, pointing to the water, "*Muma*, look, such a lot of coffee!" The color of Huangpu River indeed looked like coffee with milk.

Now the coffee in my cup again reminded me of the Huangpu River in Shanghai, a city I had left at age ten with no thought of the eventuality that I would never see it again.

§

Once, Sam's former post-doctoral researcher was staying with us while he and Sam collaborated on a project. Dave was surprised to see Sam laboriously grinding coffee by hand. "Have you ever thought of switching to an electric grinder?" he asked with great tact.

"Never," Sam answered without bothering to turn his head.

Approaching your adopted culture with your native attitude is probably inevitable for any immigrant. An electric grinder would improve efficiency, but some of the pleasure of grinding might be lost. To properly savor the rare moments of his leisure, Sam felt he needed to take his time and not rush.

However, as the years went by and hand grinding became increasingly physically challenging, Sam did switch to an electric grinder to enable him to enjoy his coffee to the last day of his life.

As for me, I went from half a cup to a quarter cup to no coffee at all years ago. Luckily, I can still walk into Starbucks, inhale deeply—a lungful even—and exclaim, "It smells heavenly!" with no discernible side effects.

21.

The Kidney Pie

Years ago, when mad cow disease first broke out on the British isles, *The New Yorker* magazine ran a cartoon depicting a cow lying on the couch, utterly despondent, while her psychiatrist tries to put a good face on the situation: "I don't think it's your fault. It's the English cooking."

English cooking does have a bad name. Tourists expect traditional English fare to be plain and boring, and they are seldom disappointed. But the natives are not complaining—they are used to it. They make a big deal of their afternoon tea, with its inevitable jams, pink cakes, and cucumber sandwiches. The rest of the time, they can supplement their steady diet of fish and chips or roast beef with superb ethnic restaurant cuisine, and they are happy. And they have something of their own they are particularly proud of. They have kidney pie.

Apparently, in cold and rainy England, kidney pie—like a large chicken potpie with kidney pieces instead of chicken—sticks to your ribs and is considered great comfort food. Over the years, it became the classic staple in the country. Outside Britain, however, many people may have heard of it, but few have encountered the genuine article. Even fewer are fond of it.

On a visit to England in the early 1970s, our family ate most of our meals at Chinese restaurants in London's Soho district. They were surprisingly good, unlike the crummy chop-suey joints in the States. The few times we did dine at an English restaurant, we never ordered the famous kidney pie.

I admit I do harbor a bit of prejudice against kidneys in general, which was acquired, of all places, in Missouri. When I was in graduate school there, one semester I roomed with Pearl (before she met and married Jim, who preferred beef *turnovers* to Chinese dumplings). Our nearby A&P regularly sold pig kidneys at bargain prices, and Pearl and I loved food at bargain prices. Besides, we both had fond memories of two very famous Chinese dishes—Stir-fried Kidneys and Golden Fried Noodles with Shrimp and Kidneys.

One day, a friend of Pearl's dropped in while we were having lunch. He was surprised to see what was on the table and inquired, "Aren't kidneys a lot of work to prepare?" Pearl said she had simply cut and stir-fried them with wine and soy sauce—not much by way of preparation. The guy almost laughed his head off. "You mean you didn't take out the ducts?" *Oh my God! You mean we've been eating kidneys with pig's urine in them?*

Needless to say, we stopped buying kidneys, bargain or not. In fact, we stopped buying any groceries, because Pearl soon fell in love with Jim and stopped coming home for meals.

Nevertheless, those ducts made an impression, and I wasn't eager to repeat the experience. I wouldn't trust anyone except the Chinese to have the patience to properly prepare kidneys, so it just made sense to stay on the safe side.

Shortly after our trip to England, we returned home to Ames. Despite the Vietnam War and its related counterculture movements, our small Midwest town remained overwhelmingly conservative and homogenous. Even if we had hankered for kidney pie, something of this nature would never have been on the menu of any restaurants in Ames. In other words, the probability of our being exposed to kidney pie was near zero.

Alas, near zero is not zero. One night, I came face-to-face with it when we were invited to dinner at our friends, the Swensons. Clayton Swenson was a colleague of Sam's who had been a Guggenheim fellow in the 1950s in Cambridge, where he met his British wife, Heather.

I was in their kitchen chatting with Heather when she removed from the oven two large golden pies exuding an enticing aroma. When Heather told me they were kidney pies, however, the ducts immediately came to mind, and my enthusiasm cooled considerably. All I could think of was how to avoid them.

Fortunately, I had learned a thing or two from Andrea. When she was in nursery school and started to boycott Chinese food, I had been furious with her. Now, however, her techniques came in handy.

Andrea essentially alternated between two strategies. The first I called *total desist*. She would rearrange the food, pushing pieces in different directions on the plate—except in the direction of her mouth. That night, I chose her second strategy: *playing favorites*. I became extraordinarily interested in salad and dinner rolls, while not completely neglecting the main entrée: choosing the crust and vegetables in the filling implied, "I'm eating it, but it just happened that my fork missed the kidney this time." Several *it just happeneds* later, when the kidney pieces became conspicuous, I exiled them to the countryside, burying them under a few leaves of salad...

Meanwhile, our fellow dinner guest obviously enjoyed the pie. He polished off a whole piece in no time and was eagerly passing his plate to Heather for a second helping. I found this a significant and encouraging sign.

Our host was also pleased, declaring with a proud smile, "It's Heather's specialty, kidney pie."

Clayton was on the verge of telling more about the dish when a loud gurgling sound suddenly came from the guest. His face turned beet red and he looked like he was in terrific pain. He quickly covered his mouth with his napkin and dashed from the table.

Such sounds from the bathroom! He was a big fellow—you'd think he was expelling the whole insides of his body! With those sounds, even if I had been served the most delicious food in the world, I wouldn't have been able to enjoy it.

I knew ox kidney was not easy to get in this neck of the woods—I certainly had never seen it—and Heather had probably special-ordered it. She went to all that trouble of making a national dish to demonstrate her hospitality and what thanks did she get? As a Brit, she was less of a foreigner in this country than Sam and me, but a foreigner just the same. I felt obliged to help her.

While Clayton and Heather did their best to pretend nothing untoward was happening, Sam and I, as if in a tacit pact, went above and beyond our duty as guests. With the accompaniment of the most unusual music, we fixed a smile on our face, held tight to our forks, and finished everything on our plates. (If you think it was easy, you should try it some time.)

I, though, did have my limits. While I acted as if everything was hunky dory, I was silently imploring the man in the bathroom: *Hurry and get out of there, please. If you keep this up any longer, I'm not going to make it.*

He finally emerged, looking remarkably calm, though a little worse for wear. Once he returned to his seat, Heather served dessert and coffee. Our dinner resumed its normal rhythm, and everybody pretended nothing was amiss, as if the bathroom episode never happened.

On the way home, Sam commented in his usual offhand way, "It didn't taste so bad; the guy was simply squeamish. If Clayton hadn't mentioned the word kidney, everything would've been fine."

I didn't answer. I was just sorry that our outstanding performances hadn't been filmed—they certainly had been worthy of an Academy Award.

22.

Cold Milk and Hot Water

American writer Margaret Halsey once recounted her experience of ordering a glass of milk in a restaurant in England.

"Milk?" The waitress was obviously taken aback.

Halsey found it a bit surprising, too. The food was horrible and she wanted a glass of milk instead. What was wrong with that? She repeated her order with emphasis, "Yes, a glass of milk."

The waitress went to the kitchen and came back empty-handed. "Please—do you wish to have your milk hot or cold?"

It was Halsey's turn to be flummoxed. Why did she have to ask? Halsey was not a baby, why would she drink hot milk? Everybody knows that even in very cold weather, cold enough to send your teeth chattering, you drink your milk cold. But this girl might be unusually dense, so Halsey simply said, "Cold."

In a little while, the waitress appeared again, this time looking extremely uncomfortable: "Do you want your milk in a porcelain cup or a glass?"

"Just roll it up in a napkin," Halsey answered.

She was, of course, being sarcastic. After her words were out and she saw how humiliated the girl was, Halsey was sorry. Before she could remedy the situation, the girl ran back to the kitchen, never to be seen again. A different waitress came to take the dessert order, and the milk incident was over.

Halsey's milk experience crossed the Atlantic Ocean in a letter to the Simon & Schuster office in New York. Her colleagues at the office had a riot; they laughed so hard they nearly choked. How could the Brits be so stupid, so unsophisticated that a glass of milk stirred up so much trouble!

This happened in the mid 1930s, around the time I was born, and I've never had the luck to set foot in the office of Simon & Schuster. If I had been there at the time, after the laughter had died down, I could have shared my experiences of ordering a cup of hot water in the United States.

To make a long story short, my relationship with beverages, whether hard or soft, with caffeine or without, has been unfortunate. Over time and for various reasons, chief among them allergies, I've had to bid a fond farewell to all beverages—except water.

America is a huge country blessed with rich resources, and obtaining a glass of water is usually not a problem. At a restaurant, a busboy will make sure your water glass is never empty. However, with the exception of coffee, Americans seem to prefer cold drinks. In a restaurant, if you ask for tea and fail to specify "hot," a huge glass of iced tea will materialize pronto. And all cold soft drinks, as well as water, are overpowered with ice, cold enough to numb your insides. In fact, by the time you finish the beverage in your glass, that three-quarters cup of ice is still there.

I'm fine with iced water in hot weather, but when it's frigid outside, just the sight of all that ice is enough to make me shiver. I must therefore gather my courage to do battle: I ask for hot water.

I grew up in China at a time when soup was always served with meals, but not water, and never iced water. But now I'm in America, and Americans drink iced water. Throughout the decades, the difference in cultural practice have made my attempts to acquire hot water in an American restaurant as hopeless as Margaret Halsey's request for cold milk in 1930s England. My situation has finally improved with the advent of globalization, but until very recently the reason for our difficulty is the same: it's simply not done.

In a typical exchange, a waiter, who might have approached me with a nice smile, would turn dubious and deeply troubled when I placed my beverage order. "Hot water?"

I understood his perspective. Hot water without coffee or a tea bag was unheard of, too weird, bordering on the bizarre. Waiters are adept at handling unexpected problems and schooled in the belief that *the customer is always right*, but all their expertise would collapse in an instant under my outrageous, unthinkable request.

However, I have always believed in education and chose my words with great care: "I have to stay away from coffee and tea for health reasons. Would you mind bringing me some hot water instead?"

But he was compelled to prevent my foolhardy behavior. Civilization absolutely depended on it. "Are you sure you don't want a tea bag?"

I was equally tenacious. "I'm positive. Once you put a tea bag in hot water, it'll be tea, and I can't drink tea."

"What about a slice of lemon then?" It was a last ditch effort, since a slice of lemon would be, like jockey shorts for a man at a public beach, far better than nothing. Understanding the proprieties, I graciously accepted the lemon.

§

My most memorable battle was fought in the 1980s. My husband and I were driving through a small town in Tennessee, when the alarm clock in his stomach inopportunely started ringing.

Sam's alarm clock rang three times a day. Like a fire alarm, it signified the dire necessity of extinguishing his hunger as soon as possible—say, within five minutes. In this case, there was only one restaurant on our side of the road, and it happened to be a fast-food joint, the kind he ordinarily tried his best to avoid. He barged in just the same, his reason indisputable: "I'm too hungry to be picky!"

The place was filled with locals who obviously had never seen *Orientals* before, and stared at us in unison with great interest. Of course, behind the counter stood a teenager ready to take our order, but apparently too young to have ever heard of hot water.

That was all right, I figured. I just had to bring her around. "You must have hot tea. Please pour me a cup from water heated for your tea."

Oh, no, she apparently knew the menu backwards—they served coffee, iced tea, Pepsi, ginger ale, Mountain Dew, and many other soft drinks, but they didn't have hot tea.

Meanwhile, my hungrier half was glaring at me meaningfully, "Don't waste any more time! For heaven's sake, just drink the ice water!"

Suddenly I saw two steaming glass pots on top of the coffeemaker behind her. The brown liquid in one pot had to be coffee, but what about the other, fabulously colorless and transparent?

"You can't drink that! It's for filtering coffee!" The girl protested.

"Of course I can," I assured her. "Why don't you give me some? I'll prove it to you right now!"

Although my tenacity won me the hot water, I discovered it wasn't very comfortable to demonstrate my otherness by drinking it under the silent, and now rather unfriendly, gaze of so many people.

§

So much of our behavior is cultural, not part of natural law. Customs that seem absolutely cool and given in one country or tribe can be considered outrageous or barbaric in a different part of the world. According to the *Free Dictionary*, uncool means "not in accord with the standards or mores of a specified group." In other words, if you are cool in one group, you may be uncool in another.

Halsey's and my experiences show that every one of us, in our own way, can be unworldly and uncool. The English waitress was provincial, but Halsey and her friends were no less so for not knowing that in England milk was always heated and stirred in tea. Similarly, American waiters reluctant to serve hot water maybe uncool, but hailing from China where tea or hot water was the order of the day, I also came across as a country bumpkin in America by not drinking iced water.

Halsey eventually wrote *With Malice Toward Some*, a memoir lampooning the British. Published in 1938, her book sold an astounding 600,000 copies. Thirty years later, Thomas Anthony Harris' self-help bible *I'm OK, You're OK* sold a whopping 15 million copies. The two volumes are poles apart, but both enjoyed great success. As a writer, I'm full of envy. I've thought of writing a book entitled *I'm Uncool, You're Uncool*, but I'm afraid it won't sell very well.

23.
Have Libretti, Will Travel

Visiting Rome in the 1960s, my parents stayed at a small hotel unfrequented by tourists. In the morning, my father ordered his breakfast in English—next, in what he improvised as pidgin English. He tried to speak slowly and enunciate each syllable distinctly. He flapped his arms, made clucking noises like a brooding hen, and then hissed to emulate the sound of eggs frying.

All to no avail. The waitress continued to shake her head with an apologetic smile. Not one given to easy defeat, my father finally got his wishes by drawing on a paper napkin—a hen in the process of parting with her oval progeny.

My mother told me this incident in the 1980s, shortly before my trip to Italy, to warn me about the formidable language problem I might encounter.

But I was not worried—not because I was great with foreign languages. When we lived in Germany one summer, on account of my faulty pronunciation, I had gone to the butcher shop asking for *half a kilo of lover* (instead of liver). Fortunately, after I stopped at each stand at an open-air market one Saturday, making known my fervent wishes to purchase a very sharp knife *to kiss the butcher* (instead of to cut the meat), no butcher was slain in that city.

But Italian was different. After all, everyone in this country speaks some Italian. Words like spaghetti, pizza, and lasagna have long become a part of English, the food they denote enriching our diet while expanding our waistlines. And many of us enjoy zucchini without stumbling over its name.

During the ensuing decades, as restaurant fare in this country grew increasingly sophisticated, some of us even broadened our

Italian vocabulary to include the likes of *Risotto con Funghi* and *Fettuccine alla Fiorentina*.

And we usually are conversant with more Italian words than those related to food. When my children were young, in order to exercise some control over the way they spent their allowance, I served as their *bank*, keeping an account book for each child. They deposited their allowance each week; withdrawals were made only with bank approval. I dubbed the practice *Bank Mama Mia*, but the kids insisted it was *Bank Mafia*.

Over the years, Sam and I learned additional Italian through osmosis. Being opera aficionados (derived from Latin, so almost an Italian word), we spent some of our leisure time poring over *libretti* (unquestionably Italian) while listening to opera records.

For instance, thanks to Figaro, who eagerly measures the bridal bed at the outset of Mozart's *The Marriage of Figaro*, we even learned a few numbers in Italian.

§

Buoyed thus by the misbegotten belief that Italian was no longer Greek to us, and despite my mother's warnings, I accompanied Sam on that trip for a conference in Bologna and a week touring the northern part of Italy.

As soon as we disembarked the train in Bologna, our luggage cart (remember those?) an overused veteran, suddenly gave up the ghost.

Of course there were no porters in sight.

Thoroughly exhausted from the long trip, we realized that, not having traveled in Europe by train for a number of years, we had forgotten how long the platforms were, and how high and steep the stairs.

During the intervening years, we had lost stamina and muscle tone, while the '80s fashion inopportunely dictated shoulder pads. Every piece of clothing came with its own set of anatomic reinforcements. These synthetic gizmos, many quite substantial, were constructed, no doubt, to masquerade as the real McCoys. Whether or not they enhance a woman's appearance is debatable, but on the road they were added weight to carry. If a single last straw is capable of breaking a camel's back, imagine what all those extra pairs of shoulders do.

With herculean effort, we managed to pull our luggage, extra shoulders and all, up the forty-odd steps of the train station, only to be confronted by several corridors with signs pointing to various exits. We chose the shortest one and found ourselves on Via Carazzi, a back street looking as if it had not seen a taxi for years.

While Sam leaned on the luggage to rest, I ventured back to the station and found the front entrance with a long line of taxis— and all non-English-speaking drivers. What a perfect opportunity for me to show off my operatic Italian!

I opened my mouth. Suddenly, the most basic words, abundant in Italian operas, such as "I," "my husband," and the verb "to be," *where did they go*? All I could manage was to stammer "*Signore…*" and "Via Carazzi…" and show the driver the crumbled slip of paper in my palm with the name of our hotel.

It wasn't much better at the restaurant later that evening, when I realized we knew how to say "poet" but not "waiter." I could articulate "tears of love" but couldn't order fruit juice. Verdi's *La Forza del Destino* prepared us to pronounce "Oh, brother, have pity on me" but not "Please help us with the menu."

We sat mesmerized, practically drowning in the ocean of words pouring from our waiter, who clearly thought that the more he spoke, the better chance we might have of understanding him. When he sensed we were truly lost, he grew more agitated, and his words tumbled out even faster. He must have repeated his speech four or five times before Sam caught the word *consiglio*.

Ah ha! Don't the two ladies in Mozart's *Così Fan Tutte* always plead *Dei consiglio* (God, counsel me) every time they get into trouble? From there Sam made the quantum leap to the lucky conclusion that the waiter was telling us to order from the full page of the chef's recommendations.

The chef was right. Both the pasta and the seafood stew were delicious. The only problem was that Sam could only tolerate one glass of wine, but the chef apparently recommended a whole liter.

Oh, well. Getting around in Italy with the help of Maestros Mozart, Verdi, and Puccini was sometimes fortuitous, other times hazardous.

Recalling the refrain *Ritorna vincitor* (return a victor) from Verdi's *Aida,* I succeeded in buying round-trip train tickets from Bologna to Venice.

Later we changed our plans and I had to return those tickets. Stumped by the clerk's rapid-fire Italian, I somehow recognized the phrase *non più.* Thanks to Musetta in Puccini's *La Boheme,* who buys the dying Mimi a hand muff, prompting the latter to sing *Non più le mani allividite* (No more will my hands be cold), I deduced that the clerk was asking me whether I was sure I no longer needed the tickets. Sadly but firmly, I repeated *Non più* and was rewarded with a refund.

However, asking directions with help from Rossini's *La Cenerentola* (*Dov'è la Tourista Officesta?*) and failing to grasp the answer, I ended up in the library of the Communist Party.

Yes, we learned the hard way that opera *libretti* were woefully inadequate in helping us negotiate the treacherous language maze—people in operas seldom eat, never need transportation, and certainly don't visit the restroom.

While the gaping holes of knowledge in those volumes left us clueless and tongue-tied on many occasions, I took comfort in the fact that some operatic expressions we did learn were never put to use, such as *D'orrore io gelo* (I'm frozen with horror), *pietà* (please spare me), and *Tutto è finito* (It's over; I'm dying).

And thanks to those libretti, we were able to bid Italy *Addio, senza rancor* (Goodbye…with no hard feelings).

24.
Danish Rye Bread

One of the pleasures of traveling to a foreign land is sampling the food it has to offer, from which, justifiably or not, you form your opinion of the country. In 1971, our family of four lived in Denmark, where Sam held a joint appointment of visiting professor at the University of Copenhagen and research physicist at Risø National Laboratory in Roskilde. We certainly did garner some unusual experiences of Danish food during our ten-month stay.

That year, Sam had an office mate at the laboratory named Nielsen. Years after we had returned to the U.S., Nielsen came to town to conduct a research project.

One evening, we invited him for dinner, and our conversation meandered to Danish food. "Do you remember our rye bread?" he asked.

Of course we did. How could we forget it? *Rugbrød*, meaning simply "buttered bread," is an extremely dark, dense sourdough rye. (Between you and me, it's also exceedingly dry, hard, and rough.) Almost daily we encountered the famous bread, as it was part of nearly every Danish meal, from the quotidian lunch box to the black-tie banquet.

I had even attended a demonstration once that year to learn the secret of making *smørrebrød,* the quintessentially Danish open sandwich. You start with a square piece of rye bread about one-third of an inch thick. After cutting it vertically into two rectangles, you smear each half with butter of equal thickness (the demonstrator emphasized *equal*), and cover with lettuce and ham or anything edible you care to have. You have now made two *smørrebrød.*

Two rectangular pieces of *smørrebrød* constitute a typical lunch.

From a three-year-old to a 200-pound man, everyone gets two pieces, equivalent to one piece of rye bread with butter and... whatever else is on it.

The *whatever* runs the gamut, and can often be eyebrow-raising. For instance, Sam's office mate at the University of Copenhagen would eat his potato or egg *smørrebrød* for lunch with great relish. As if they were endowed with magic, the two tiny pieces sustained the man all afternoon. This Dane would boil a single potato or egg in the morning for the topping of both his and his wife's lunch—true gender equality.

Andrea, who was in a Danish school that year, told us that when her best friend bit into her chocolate *smørrebrød*, the thin pieces of chocolate bar made an agreeable crunching sound. On other days, the topping might be a couple of banana slices.

At banquets, you would find a long table laden with *smørrebrød* topped with a variety of riches such as caviar, baby shrimp, ham, pickled herring, cucumber, cheese, or liverwurst... always with the same butter and bread, of course.

Not only Denmark, but also Sweden and Norway—all of Scandinavia can't seem to live without their *smørrebrød*.

§

Before we left for Denmark, we already knew that it was a neighbor of the Arctic Circle, with long winters and short summers. When we arrived at the end of September, winter was already beginning, with long nights and short days. Soon, daybreak didn't arrive until ten o'clock in the morning, and streetlights were lit by three. When I walked Clif to school in the morning and back in the afternoon, the streets were full of cars and people rushing about their daily business, but it was black like midnight—truly surreal. The so-called daylight, from ten to three, was similar to dusk. In other words, for twenty-four hours a day, the difference between day and night was only a matter of degree of darkness, or a matter of opinion.

The difference was further diminished by the cloudy weather. From September to May, sunshine was like the smile of Cinderella's wicked stepmother; you might crave it but you'd never see it. We didn't see it once.

During those interminably cold, dark, and dreary days, I yearned for comfort food—something hot, soft, and moist—but *smørrebrød* was just the opposite. You might say it's an acquired taste—a taste that I never acquired. In fact, I came to nurture quite a grudge against Denmark's proud national dish. For the sake of politeness, however, I never revealed my unfortunate attitude to my Danish friends.

So when Nielsen asked about the rye bread that night at dinner, I could only nod vaguely and reply, "Yes, of course I remember."

Nielsen told us he had looked all over Oak Ridge but was unable to find Danish rye bread. He had even searched Knoxville, still with no luck. I nodded with great sympathy. As far as I knew, there wasn't anything in either city that had the texture and taste of Danish rye bread. And I understood what it was like to crave a certain food without possibility of finding it.

Nielsen missed the bread so much that he decided to learn to make it himself—after all, he was an experimental physicist—and after repeated attempts, he finally succeeded. Now he no longer had the acute problem of not having the right bread for his *smørrebrød*. He was so proud that he was ready to divulge the secret of his months of research on rye bread, when Sam cut him off: "Speaking of Danish rye bread, it reminds me of what happened to us in Denmark…"

Uh, oh. I knew the story he was going to tell. Although it was a true story, no Dane would appreciate hearing it. I was sitting too far away to kick him under the table, so I warned him with a hard glare. But he deliberately ignored me and went on with the story.

When Andrea and Clif started school in Denmark, naturally, they wanted to be just like the other kids, eating *smørrebrød* for lunch. Every week I would buy one short loaf of Danish rye bread, use one slice per child, and top it with ham or liverwurst. It was easy enough.

One day I was surprised to find the loaf I had bought wasn't in slices. A look at the package confirmed that it wasn't pre-sliced—I had gotten the wrong kind. No big deal, I figured; I could simply cut it myself.

Well, not only could I *not* slice it, I couldn't make a dent in it in any way. It was like a fossil. Then Sam tried, also no luck.

Okay, we would do it together. I held our sharpest kitchen knife on top of the loaf with both hands, while Sam hit the knife with a hammer. My wrists suffered from the shock of the impact, the knife was badly chipped, but the bread was undamaged.

We gave up and went out to buy the sliced kind.

I was ready to throw the indestructible loaf in the garbage when I thought of a way to salvage the situation. Our German friends used to feed ducks in the park with their leftover bread. I thought our kids might enjoy feeding the bread to the ducks in the lake at a nearby park. A nice way to celebrate spring.

At the park, since we knew it was impossible to break the bread with our hands, Sam found a rock of appropriate shape by the side of the lake to knock on the bread.

No dice.

He then tried to hit the bread on a huge boulder. Like our knife at home, the rock lost—a piece of it broke off.

Thereupon Sam lost his temper—patience was never one of his strong suits—and threw the whole loaf in the lake. Danish ducks seemed to know the bread well; not one came forward to claim a piece of it.

"That loaf of bread sank straight to the bottom. It was more than ten years ago, and as far as we know, it's still reposing undisturbed in that lake!"

Sam had a hearty laugh. The other of our two guests that night, a Greek colleague, also chuckled.

Only Nielsen looked sour, and he never mentioned his beloved rye bread again.

25.
Starving in Copenhagen

If *smørrebrød* was the most important and popular food in Denmark, hot dogs were not far behind. The Danes call them *rød pølse,* red sausage. They were sold everywhere, even from carts on street corners, and appeared at all outdoor activities and informal social functions. I was told that in Denmark—a country of five million at the time—more than 100 million red sausages were consumed every year.

With a history of being averse to American hot dogs, I was further alienated by the fact that the Danish ones were dyed a uniformly bright red color, another of my pet peeves. They were typically served with an artificial, bright yellow *orange* soda, which was the nonalcoholic byproduct of the Danish beer-making process. Since every school activity and children's birthday party always featured red sausage and orange soda, I was heartsick that I couldn't protect my kids from junk food that year.

On the bright side, in contrast to the rye bread, Denmark also had *wienerbrød.* Introduced in 1840 by Viennese chefs, *wienerbrød* are pastries that come in various shapes and flavors, with or without fruit, all of them delicate, multi-layered, and heavenly. I was surprised to learn that the Danes in turn brought them to America in the early 1920s, and they are now known all over the country as *Danish* pastry. Perhaps too much was lost in translation or during the difficult transatlantic voyage, but to call the American version Danish pastry is equivalent to identifying chop-suey as Chinese food, both laughable and insulting.

An American woman who lived across the street from us in Roskilde refused to touch *wienerbrød,* declaring, "It's too rich!

Squeeze it and you'll get four ounces of butter!" I didn't doubt she was right, but whenever I encountered a piece, my overwhelming desire was to savor it. Besides, what could I have done with all that butter anyway?

It seemed that all the money and energy the Danes saved from eating mostly open sandwiches and red sausages they poured into their exquisite sweets. They were all far superior to their American counterparts.

These treats were often present at the Danish afternoon tea, which was a serious affair. The hostess would serve as many as three or four of her specialties, among them usually a fruit tart—cake with pieces of apple, strawberry, or plum on top—a feast for all your senses. Tea generally began at three o'clock, lingered till almost six, and concluded with a slowly-sipped sherry.

§

Despite the delectable baked goods, what stands out in my memory of our year in Denmark is a series of episodes in which we suffered hunger—beginning with our very first day there.

We arrived in Copenhagen just before classes started at the university. Due to a last-minute change in the flight schedule, we were a day late, but were delighted to find a car sent by the Roskilde lab waiting for us.

I had hoped to learn some Danish before we left, but my only Danish friend in Ames had told me not to bother, assuring me that "everybody in Denmark speaks English." But that driver, the first Dane we met, immediately proved her wrong. We peppered him with questions—we were so curious about everything—and he could only respond in Danish with an apologetic smile. He dropped us at our house (one of several guesthouses provided by the Lab for visiting staff) in Roskilde, murmured something and left us.

The unit was ranch-style, simple but adequate, with furniture, linens, pots and pans, and dishes. In the kitchen, the tiny refrigerator had a tray of ice cubes, and the cupboards were empty except for a half-filled shaker of salt. By then, it was very dark outside, and we were very hungry.

We tried to call information to locate a food shop or restaurant, but the Danish phone system was a mystery that we tried but failed to solve, so Sam ventured out on foot in search of dinner. He looked left and right, chose right, walked a couple of miles, and found a gas station that sold—what do you expect? Red sausage. Our first meal in Denmark.

Later we learned that Allen, a former colleague of Sam's in Ames who was the director of the lab, had planned to take us out for dinner but had gone to the wrong house. Leaving a bag of apples at the doorstep as a welcome gift, he had gone home, perhaps assuming we would arrive on a different day. We never found out who enjoyed the apples.

Coincidently, we had two other hunger episodes that involved Allen. Back in Ames one evening, Allen and his Danish wife Jette had invited us for beef fondue. I had no idea what beef fondue was, but it sounded exotic. And the anticipation of an introduction to Danish cuisine filled me with high hopes.

Next to the candles and flowers on the table was a big platter of cubed, lean, raw beef. A small copper pot, polished to a shine, was half filled with oil. We sat at the table drinking wine, visiting, and waiting for the oil to be heated by the burner under the pot. When it was ready, we each used a different colored, long-handled steel fork to cook our beef.

Call me a pessimist, but coming from the East, where people seem to be more adept at achieving maximal results with minimal resources, I had a feeling the dinner wasn't going to turn out well. The beef was entirely *au naturel*, meaning unseasoned and flavorless. The oil was lukewarm at best, and all the forks dipping into it only reduced its temperature further. Timing was impossible. The meat would either turn out gray on the outside and red inside—still largely raw—or overcooked with a texture of shoe leather. I didn't know about the others, but Sam and I went home hungry that night.

I couldn't help comparing that beef fondue to the hotpot, *huo-guo*, that I grew up with. The meat—beef, pork, lamb, and chicken—was cut into paper-thin slices. It cooked instantly when plunged into delicious, furiously boiling broth, and was eaten with a variety of sauces or left simmering in the soup with tofu, vegetables, and an infinite number of goodies. *Huo-guo* made an immensely satisfying meal on cold winter nights.

Shortly after we arrived in Denmark, we were invited to Allen's house for dinner. I hoped Jette, now back in her home country, would serve some Danish specialty, but it was the unfortunate beef fondue again. Perhaps beef fondue was a Danish specialty from the Viking days. It was the only time in my life I wished for *smørrebrød*.

§

The Danes were crazy about their alcohol, especially beer. In the middle of December, Ørsted Institute held its annual Christmas lunch, spouses not included. As the cost per person was roughly seven times the average restaurant lunch, Sam was looking forward to a great Danish feast.

When he got there punctually at noon, the auditorium's huge table was crowded with people, from the director of the institute, professors, and graduate students to the staff and secretaries. Everyone was already having a fabulous time, talking and laughing.

The table was conspicuously bare—no plates, silverware, or napkins; no potato chips, cheese, or crackers. (Incidentally, the Danes do eat potato chips. I found some in our neighborhood supermarket flavored with dill. They were delicious.)

In front of every person, however, were two glasses: a large one for beer, a small one for *snaps*. *Snaps* is the famous Danish hard liquor, with an alcohol content on par with the Chinese *Maotai*, the drink served to President Nixon during his historic visit to China. (Good *Maotai* should ignite when you strike a match to it.)

Numerous waiters were busy filling the glasses, never allowing them to remain even half empty. From time to time, some people would leave their seats with their *snaps* to toast you by saying "*Skol*," the Danish equivalent of "Cheers!" Sam was much relieved that the Danes didn't force him to go "Bottoms up" like the Chinese.

For two hours, waiters came with large trays full of *snaps* and beer and left with empty bottles. After several hundred empty bottles had been taken away, there was still no food. Sam, still carefully nursing his first glasses of beer and *snaps*, began to feel quite anxious. His neighbors assured him, "Don't worry! Plenty of great food will be here in a jiffy!"

Eventually food did arrive—one *smørrebrød* per person, the typical small piece of open sandwich on a tiny plate.

The appetizer was here, Sam reasoned, how could the rest be far away? He ate his sandwich and settled down to wait. A whole sixty minutes later, at half past three, came the second course: another *smørrebrød*.

People were still talking, laughing, and drinking; everything was hunky-dory. By five o'clock, the number of empty bottles had reached the thousands. The room was filled with couples dancing, the atmosphere growing even more festive.

Sam's stomach, however, was feeling less and less festive. He decided to leave the party and go home for a real meal.

§

What bothered us the most after settling down in Roskilde was the appalling lack of vegetables. The situation was bad enough in America, where people seemed to care a great deal about meat and dessert, while vegetables were present merely for decoration. After fulfilling their ceremonial function, they usually ended up in the garbage can. Although the situation has improved over the years, compared to the abundance of myriad green leafy vegetables in China, the vegetable selection in most of America is still worse than pathetic.

The Danes, however, didn't seem to need any vegetables whatsoever, not even for decoration. Even common spinach and broccoli couldn't be found. Any cabbage and Brussels sprouts that might show up in the produce aisle looked like soldiers just returned from the battlefield: gaunt, exhausted, badly injured, and full of holes.

All winter long, I came back from every shopping trip with the same three vegetables—cucumbers, lettuce, and mushrooms. The cucumbers were yellowish green, longer than a foot, and disgustingly soft in texture. I can't begin to speculate the reason for the softness. Danish preference? Past retirement age? Only one kind of lettuce was available—butter lettuce, bland as iceberg lettuce sans the crispness. The mushrooms were small and white, perhaps specially cultivated to fit on top of their *smørrebrød*.

One day at the cafeteria, Sam and another physicist (an Argentine-American) were grumbling about the scarcity of vegetables in Denmark. A Danish colleague was offended, "How can you say we don't have vegetables? We have potatoes!"

At a party one night, I was ecstatic to learn about a farmers market that took place Wednesday and Saturday mornings in front of the cathedral in Roskilde. I got up early on Wednesday morning, and was thrilled to see from far away quite a few stands with green leaves!

Breathless when I reached the stands, I was devastated to discover that the green leaves were merely potted plants. Ever tenacious, I searched each stand but found only the same tired vegetables available at the grocery store. The only difference was that they looked like they had been imported from the Isle of Lilliput the year before and had turned translucent in the freezing wind.

When spring finally sprang, I was surprised one day to come upon a basket full of greens in a small store. By God, was that spinach? My first sighting of spinach in Denmark! I had thought the Danes didn't eat spinach!

The owner asked, "How much?"

I looked around, my heart racing. No one seemed to be interested in this rare and precious find. I quickly replied, "All of it!"

He was taken aback, and other customers looked askance at me, but what did I care? What euphoria to cart a kilo of spinach home!

§

Easter was an important holiday in Denmark, a four-day weekend. We had planned to take advantage of that Thursday off to buy our children some spring clothes.

The intended Thursday shopping excursion was particularly important for us because it was a rare occasion that Sam would be available to drive us. He was the only one who knew how to drive a standard-transmission car, but all Danish stores closed their doors promptly at five—long before he got off work. This meant I typically went shopping alone nearly every day on foot, carrying home groceries for our family of four. Buying anything out of walking distance was out of the question.

That first morning of the Easter holiday, we realized right away something was wrong: The streets were unusually quiet, and every storefront was dark. Could it be true? They were all closed for the holiday weekend!

Our clothes-shopping plans were clearly out the window, but we weren't too worried about food. After all, it was Thursday. Markets wouldn't close on a weekday, would they?

Yes, they would, and yes, they had. Their windows cheerfully and temptingly displayed chunks of cheese and bottles of wine, but their doors were locked. More alarmingly, all restaurants and cafes were closed, and not even a single red sausage wagon was in sight. Neon signs everywhere were dark.

We were reduced to the grim task of surviving on the contents of our refrigerator. That tiny box would have been fine for a bachelor who ate out every day and needed to chill an occasional bottle of wine. Our family of four with two growing children, however, didn't have enough food in the fridge to last one day, not to mention four.

We considered driving to Hamburg, Germany, the nearest big city outside of Denmark, but thought better of it—by the time we arrived, stores in Germany would be closed, too.

We ate up everything in the fridge, including a quarter jar of mayonnaise, then stayed hungry until Friday afternoon when we heard of one bakery that was mercifully open for a couple of hours. It was doing great business, but only bread and eggs were available by the time we rushed there. A lone small carton of milk sat in the store refrigerator with a note attached—*sold*.

Our situation, however, improved drastically on Saturday, for we discovered that several markets deigned to open for half a day. That evening, after being famished for days, we indulged ourselves with an unusually big dinner. Overfed and happy, Sam and I made our leisurely way to a party given by one of Sam's Danish colleagues.

The Danes were extremely punctual for dinners, but parties were informal like American ones—umpteen guests, some arriving late and others leaving early. The party was supposed to start at seven o'clock; we reached our destination shortly after nine, when the party should have been in full swing.

Instead of a houseful of guests, only three couples sat in the living room, looking as if they had been waiting for a long time. Our host and hostess seemed to be in a hurry—they immediately ushered us to the dining room and seated us at the table, and in a matter of minutes, we were served dinner!

This was a party?

When our Danish host had invited us to a *party*, we took him literally, not realizing that he actually meant *dinner*. More unforgivable was that, being visitors from America, we were the honored guests that night, and the entrée was an unusually extravagant roasted leg of lamb, which had turned hard and tough from being kept warm in the oven for hours.

Now how could we tell our hosts that we had just had a big dinner at home—and why?

And after so many months of disappointing food, we missed our once-in-a-lifetime opportunity to enjoy what would have been a fantastic leg of lamb dinner!

26.

Pork Stories

There is a funny story about pork that is well known in China, and it never fails to get a laugh when told. I like it especially because it's about food, but doesn't involve cooking.

One lucky day, the father of a destitute family manages to bring home a small piece of salted pork, but it's too small for everyone to get a taste. Come mealtime, he nails the pork on the wall. Everyone is supposed to take a look at the pork, imagine eating it, and then swallow a mouthful of rice. That works pretty well until the five-year-old yells out: "Papa, Papa, Second Older Brother is cheating! Each time before eating his rice he looks twice at the pork!"

The kid is taking *waste not, want not* to a new level, and I like to call this story The Twice-Looked Pork.

My own pork story is quite different.

Not long after Sam's retirement, and after more than forty years of marriage, he mentioned during dinner one evening that he married me for my pork dish—stir-fried pork with onions, to be exact. He said I had made it for him once, on the first occasion we dined together shortly after we met, and he had imagined how nice it would be if he could have that dish regularly.

This was not the first time he had given a reason for marrying me. A few years after he began working at the Oak Ridge National Laboratory, I was recruited there as a technical editor. The lab was a predictably bureaucratic government institution, and one day they required the employees in my department to fill out a form listing three of our strengths.

I was stumped, unable to come up with a single thing I thought I particularly excelled at. At dinner I told Sam my predicament and was surprised that he said he knew the answers. I have since forgotten the other two, but the first strength he mentioned caught my attention. He married me for my intelligence, he said, because he wanted intelligent children. At the time, we had been married more than thirty years and this was the first time he told me point-blank why he married me. Instead of feeling flattered, I was astounded that he was so calculating. When I married him, I certainly wasn't thinking about children, intelligent ones or otherwise. He made me feel like a Yorkshire pig, chosen and bred for her functionality.

It was some ten years later that Sam mentioned the pork dish. Again, it was news to me and less than complimentary. I couldn't tell whether he was joking. It seemed quite a silly reason to marry someone, and his remark came out of the blue. In all those years, he had never even given me one clue that he was particularly fond of that dish.

I only vaguely remembered the mundane shredded pork stir-fried with onions I served the night Sam stayed for dinner after helping my brother Charley assemble his new bicycle. It was my first summer in this country. Working as a typist and staying with Charley, I had learned a few rudimentary cooking skills from my brother by that time. Since Charley and Sam were busy working with the bike, I made dinner using whatever I could find in the refrigerator.

Sam was the first person I met in Iowa when I arrived from Oregon that summer, but it wasn't until we were both in New York two years later that we began to see each other. We got married the following summer, and shortly afterwards he grew grievously ill with ulcers brought on by work pressures. I knew nothing about ulcers, let alone that anyone could be so sick from them. The prevailing medical treatment at the time was tranquilizers and a bland diet to neutralize the gastric acid. All condiments were strictly forbidden, including onion and garlic. I took it seriously and learned to cook without them.

While his ulcers remained a serious recurring health issue all his life, medical research later exonerated many trigger foods, and he was allowed all types of seasonings again. By then years had gone by, and I discovered to my dismay that, having banned onion and garlic from the kitchen for too long, I had become allergic to them.

It was ironic that while Sam could eat almost everything without restriction, even fried onion rings, I now had to assiduously avoid onion and garlic, among many other items on my ever-lengthening list of food allergies.

In short, the circumstances were such that I hadn't made stir-fried pork with onions since that summer night in Iowa in 1958. Even after he mentioned it as the reason he married me, I didn't take him seriously. I still didn't make that dish, and he seemed to forget all about it, just as before.

A couple of years later, after a visit from Andrea, Doug, and our two granddaughters, I found a small onion in the refrigerator left over from a meal they had prepared. That lone onion sat in the vegetable bin for a few months, until it occurred to me to stir-fry it with pork. Since I was still allergic to onion, I only ate a little of the dish. Sam, however, polished it off readily, and with great relish. For some reason, neither of us made any mention of the occasion.

Sam died from massive cerebral hemorrhage that night.

Days later it suddenly occurred to me that the pork dish that he claimed that he married me for had been our last meal together, forty-seven years after our first.

Sam was gone, leaving me with questions I still ponder occasionally, among them the two determinedly unsentimental *reasons* he married me. At the time, he seemed anything but unsentimental. Wouldn't I have sensed it if someone had married me in cold blood?

I know people are never two-dimensional; they are complicated, and their feelings change over time. Relationships between husband and wife are even more complicated, and also change over time. Our marriage was no exception. Love, like everything else, doesn't last forever, and perhaps it mutates into appreciation of peripheral attributes, like intelligence and the ability to cook a pork dish. Was that what happened to us?

Thus, I've been plagued by not a small amount of soul-searching:

how well did I know the man I was married to for forty-four years?
Not much. Not very much at all.
Do many marriages end with question marks, or just mine?

27.
I Survived My Daughter's Kitchen

When Andrea was five years old, she announced to me one day, in all seriousness: "Mommy, I've made up my mind. When I grow up, I won't get married and I'll always live with you and Daddy!"

I'm usually slow in reacting, but for some reason that time I was quick, "That'll be great! Don't you go back on your word! I'll tell you what—let me put it in writing for you. Since you don't know how to sign your name, we'll just use your fingerprint instead."

The Chinese have an expression: *A girl will change eighteen times before she reaches womanhood.* Andrea changed from a strong-minded little girl who couldn't wait to tell me all about what happened at school every day, to the conscientious student who excelled in every subject and helped at home by shopping for groceries every week, cleaning up the kitchen with her brother every night, and taking over cooking family dinners when necessary.

She was never fazed by tasks that I found daunting, like doing calculus, reading music, and deciphering sewing patterns. I never tired of listening to her practicing the piano, and we loved shopping for clothes together, for we are drawn to the same colors and styles.

Most remarkably, Andrea seemed to have skipped the requisite rebellious teenage period. When she was seventeen, it struck a hole in my heart when she went away to UC Berkeley, two thousand miles away. Sam and I were both teaching at the time and couldn't get away, but we talked to her every day on the phone and racked up horrendous monthly long distance bills.

Not surprisingly, her promise to live with us forever, like the small security blanket she carried as a toddler, had long disappeared without a trace.

Eventually, her resolve to not get married evolved to *marry, but no children*; twenty years after her initial statement, she was ready to tie the knot.

Since her future in-laws lived more than a thousand miles away, we didn't meet them until the night before the wedding. It so happened Doug's mother was eager for grandchildren and somehow had learned about Andrea's resolve to forego having kids. Almost immediately after we met, she began to recruit me to change Andrea's mind. Knowing Andrea, I felt there wasn't much I could do and suggested she lobby the bridegroom instead.

Ten years went by, during which the young couple devoted their energies to their respective careers and were successful and productive—except in terms of reproduction. Most of their friends were already promoted to parenthood, but not these two. I didn't know how Doug's mother felt, but my father started to get antsy. More than a traditional Chinese patriarch, he would only recognize his son's children as his true grandchildren, so whether Andrea had children or not shouldn't have been a concern of his. But he could never miss a chance to assert his authority, and naturally he assumed it had to be my fault: "Your daughter has been married for ten years with no kids, and you're not doing anything about it?"

As usual, I tried my best to placate him. "I'm afraid there's not much I can do. They're extremely busy. Perhaps they think they don't have time to bring up a baby."

"Nonsense! You can always go live with them and help!"

Yeah, that's my father all right, always generous with my *time.* Nevertheless, I felt obliged to explain: "Young people are very different nowadays. Even if I offered, I doubt they'd take me up on it."

As it turned out, this exchange was unnecessary. Shortly after, came the exciting news that Andrea had changed her mind. It was going to be a girl, to be named Sylvia.

Sylvia, I thought, *what a beautiful name!*

Andrea told me Shubert had set to music a poem with the same name by Shakespeare. She and Doug bought half a dozen versions of the song on CD and played them every day, so that Sylvia would be familiar with it prenatally.

And that was not all. Extremely busy as the parents-to-be were, they took time every week to attend classes on natural childbirth and were reading nearly twenty books on pregnancy and childcare. Obviously, no effort was spared in giving the baby a fabulous beginning.

They really put me to shame. Sam and I did nothing of the kind during my pregnancy, and didn't know anyone who did. Like everyone else, we were never very focused on preparing for parenthood, and I admit we were a little worse than most. Confucius famously says *renwu yuanlu, biyou jinyou*: he who doesn't worry about the future is bound to suffer from problems of here and now. Both Sam and I belong to that unfortunate category.

While I was pregnant with Andrea, we were living north of New York City, in Mount Kisco. I worked until Friday, a week before her due date, and we went to a dinner party at my cousin's apartment in New York City the following day.

At the party, several friends were appalled that we hadn't yet purchased a copy of the authoritative guide for new parents, Dr. Benjamin Spock's *Baby and Child Care, and* advised us to do so immediately.

Bookstores were closed that time of night, but it wasn't a problem—the book was also sold at drugstores. We started our search methodically near my cousin's apartment, Sam double-parking as I waddled unsteadily into the store. I don't remember how many places we tried, but either the stores were just closing or the book was sold out. We went home near midnight empty-handed.

Perhaps getting in and out of the car too many times had something to do with it. Less than an hour after we reached home, my labor began, and Andrea was born at seven o'clock in the morning.

I wasn't proud of myself when I told Andrea this story. My feelings were complicated. Despite being sheepish for failing to be a model mother, I was a bit defensive—*your parents might not be very conscientious, but you turned out okay, didn't you?* I was also harboring the innate protective feeling a mother has toward her offspring. I felt she was overdoing it; she could use more rest. And I felt sad that times had changed so much in one generation.

As a matter of fact, the differences between Andrea's attitude towards parenthood and mine were more than generational. I was brought up to expect a roof over my head, food to eat, and a school to attend, but I was never my parents' priority. Nobody ever made a fuss about me. That cultural attitude was reflected in my behavior as a parent. Now I had to adjust to Andrea's way of preparing for parenthood at a different time in a different culture, where a child is the most important thing in their lives.

My complicated feelings didn't stand in the way of my absorbing new knowledge, however. From Andrea, this grandmother-to-be learned a great deal about modern pregnancy and natural childbirth. I was told she intended to have the baby without a single drop of anesthesia, and we didn't need to go to the hospital to help. In addition to Doug and her obstetrician, they would have a doula there.

I was flummoxed. "Doula? What's a doula?"

It turned out a doula is not a nurse or a midwife, but an expert in natural childbirth, present solely to provide assistance and support.

I tried it on my Chinese-American friends; their answers were identical: "Doula? What's a doula?"

Aha! I was not the only one who was behind times.

That was when I understood that none of us sets out intentionally to be ignorant, unaware. I, for one, read papers and watch television, trying my best to keep abreast of the new, but time has a way of speeding up, leaving me far behind—in the dust.

§

The baby's due date came and went. It was another eight days when the news finally came: the parents-to-be and their doula were leaving for the hospital. The phone call was like a shot of adrenaline for Sam and me. Our heads became muddled; we couldn't concentrate on anything, couldn't eat or sleep.

Entrusted with the all-important job of providing sustenance for Andrea and Doug after they returned from the hospital, we were ready and eager to make our drive from San Diego to Los Angeles—contrary to the best judgment of many our local Chinese-American friends.

Our friends could be roughly divided into two camps. The first group expressed their concerns for me and tried to dissuade me from going: "Let's face it, you hate to cook and have problems serving meals for two. Why would you take on the challenge of doing it for four?" Or, "The young generation usually manage quite well by themselves. In your physical condition, you should thank your lucky stars that *you* don't need help right now."

What they said did make sense, and I knew better than anyone else my own deplorable lack of physical strength and culinary skills. This time, however, my mind was made up. I beat my chest, declaring: "At home, I'm constantly distracted by things I want to do other than cooking. Over there, I'll simply focus on the three meals. I think I can manage that much."

Actually, my courage was fortified for an additional reason, a reason that I was a bit ashamed to divulge: I was counting on Sam as my *assistant*. This so-called assistant was not a volunteer, of course. He would have loved to stay out of the kitchen, but often found it necessary to pitch in, and gradually had gotten accustomed to helping. His skills slowly grew from those of an assistant to semi-cook, and I had high hopes that the prefix would be dropped entirely some day.

He was like an answer sheet in my pocket at an exam—it made me feel better prepared. (As it turned out, he got sick the day after we arrived in Los Angeles and was of no help whatsoever.)

The second group was more pragmatic; they said if I were determined to go, I should first learn something about *zuoyuezi*.

Zuoyuezi, literally "sitting the month," is the traditional Chinese regimen following childbirth, which includes mandatory bed rest for the mother for thirty days, and many food requirements and restrictions. I knew something about it, of course, but never paid much attention to it, and thought it had long disappeared with foot-binding and red-painted wooden chamber pots. Back in the 1960s when my friends and I had our babies in this country, we never knew of anyone practicing *zuoyuezi*. With wars and other calamities devastating the country, even my mother and her generation had abandoned the luxury.

The reason my friends and I didn't follow the custom was

obvious: it was impractical here, if not impossible. In China, you always had help from either servants or family, so a whole month's confinement was not a problem. At the hospital in this country, they make you get out of bed and walk the very same day. In my case, when we returned home with our baby, we didn't know anyone who could lend a hand.

More importantly, people in this country seemed to be incredibly hardy. In fact, a friend of mine saw a woman do pushups on the cold cement floor of their shared hospital room almost immediately after giving birth. With those tough Caucasian women as our friends and neighbors, how could we have stayed in bed even if we had help?

Who would guess that thirty years later, along with natural childbirth and breastfeeding, *zuoyuezi* was also enjoying a renaissance, and some of my friends in San Diego were actually quite knowledgeable about it. Though I knew nothing about natural childbirth and breastfeeding, I thought I could learn something about *zuoyuezi*, thereby making my humble contribution as a grandmother.

The list of dos and don'ts during the postpartum month of *zuoyuezi* is long, including a ban on bending over, bathing, washing hair, and crying. (For the mother, not the baby, of course. Birth mother crying is considered a bad omen and not conducive to recovery.)

Needless to say, food is of the utmost importance. Eating and drinking anything raw or cold is taboo, and different geographical regions in China dictate different foods for recovery and lactation stimulation. In Taiwan, the famous Sesame Oil Chicken is stewed with a lot of ginger and a whole bottle of rice wine, but no salt or water. It's believed that the alcohol in the wine will mostly evaporate and that the remaining residue will be especially beneficial for a new mother. Sesame oil is added the last minute, its aroma ensuring a good appetite. The Cantonese believe in pork feet soup with a whole bottle of red vinegar—again, no salt, no water. The provinces south of the Yangtze River use a pair of hens for soup, plus meat bones, red dates, dried longan (a tropical fruit, cousin to lychee) and Western ginseng.

I began to feel sorry for myself for having given birth to two children but never having enjoyed Sesame Oil Chicken or the other restorative dishes. I may have missed out, but it wasn't too late for Andrea. Besides, considering the difference of our physical constitution with that of the Caucasians, I thought staying away from anything exceedingly cold might be a good idea. And a diet rich in fruits and vegetables couldn't be anything but healing for post-partum.

I should have known the antiquated regimen would not appeal to Andrea, but I thought it was worth a try. Sam and I stuffed our trunk with rice wine, red vinegar, dried shiitake mushrooms, red dates, soybeans, and all manner of fresh vegetables and fruits, and headed north to Los Angeles.

§

Sylvia's charm was truly captivating. She had a full head of black hair, pink complexion, sparkling eyes, straight nose, and ten small fingers like tender shoots.

Andrea was breastfeeding when we arrived. When I saw her half bottle of water and half-eaten sandwich, I tried to mention casually, "The Chinese custom is no cold or raw foods or drinks."

"I had no choice in the hospital—I would have starved and gotten dehydrated," she said. She was defensive, and she was right. We would just have to do what we could from now on.

The new parents reminded me of soldiers in the trenches. They seemed to have no time or inclination to eat or sleep. All their energies were focused on breastfeeding, which was not going very smoothly. It didn't take me long to realize there wasn't much I could do to help. All the *zuoyuezi* stuff suddenly seemed quite irrelevant; I retreated to the kitchen.

I began by putting the food we brought into their cupboards and refrigerator. When I saw what was there, my heart sank.

God knows I was never good at planning ahead, but I did give a lot of thought to bringing up my kids—particularly about fostering their interest in Chinese food.

As I mentioned earlier, many Chinese-American children have problems with foods that are not mainstream American, such as pork tripe, fermented vegetables, and wood ear mushrooms. (I still remember, as a child after the war, gathering the fresh, crunchy, delicate-flavored ground ear mushrooms that would sprout from the yard after a rain. Ground ear is similar to wood ear but not found in the U.S.)

Unfortunately, what is so much a part of my fond childhood memories is a source of ridicule to children growing up in this land. They make faces or make fun of them, or simply refuse to eat them. Those kids also tend to avoid and look down on, anything Chinese.

As a mother determined to prevent such behavior, I fed Andrea Chinese food as soon as she was on solids, and successfully quelled her ensuing rebellion. When it was Clifton's time, he got Chinese food processed in a blender instead of bottled baby food.

I thought by taking such precautions, we wouldn't have any generation or culture gap when they grew up—at least not in the kitchen. But as I perused the contents of Andrea's cupboards and refrigerator, I had to admit I had been terribly naïve. The gaps between us were wide and deep, like Yangtze River or the Mississippi, if you will.

True, both my kids were brought up on Chinese food, so they never pulled a long face when they encountered wood ear and the like; they actually enjoyed eating them. But that turned out to be not even half the battle, for in Andrea's kitchen I saw sausages from Provence, goose liver pâté, Arborio risotto rice, and porcini mushrooms. If we believe *we are what we eat*, then the owners of that kitchen had to be of French and Italian descent!

And the dried foods in her pantry were all *sun-dried*. Frankly, I wasn't aware of any other way of drying. When I was growing up in China, fish, soybeans, strips of radish, wet laundry—everything was sun-dried. What was so great about that? In my day, it just meant being dried by the street, covered with a thin layer of dust. Who would think that many years later, sun-dried foods would be touted as *gourmet*, commanding outrageously higher prices?

When I put my thoughts aside and got ready to start cooking that day, however, I came upon a less philosophical problem—I couldn't find any salt. After searching, I did manage to locate a small container of Kosher Gourmet Coarse Salt. Having used plain Morton salt for more than thirty years, I hadn't noticed salt even came in other brands, could be gourmet or plain, kosher or not, coarse or fine. The only coarse salt I knew came in huge sacks to spread on the snowy streets of Iowa and Tennessee. When did it become gourmet?

Which goes to show that I had been unaware of my basic problem—inferior salt. No wonder my cooking was not up to par! With this secret weapon now at my disposal, finally I would get to turn over a new leaf and impress everyone with my culinary skills.

Alas, the gourmet coarse salt, when dropped in hot oil, sank straight to the bottom and stayed there. My heart dropped, too. Apparently coarse salt could melt snow, but hot oil couldn't melt coarse salt. And what did that gourmet salt taste like? I wouldn't know, for it seemed to have no taste, least of all salty.

The Chinese have an expression—*Even a clever woman can't cook without rice.* The same goes for salt. I would have to somehow get by for this meal and ask my *assistant* to buy some the next day.

Then there was another hurdle: Andrea's stove. The professional Viking gas range was truly powerful, but I took one look and thought, *Uh, oh.*

In *Under the Tuscan Sun*, writer Frances Mayes describes the primitive equipment in the kitchen of a rural villa in Tuscany she had bought on an impulse. In comparison, she writes, the restaurant-class cooking range in her San Francisco house appears to be so huge and such a super technological marvel, that it looks ready to take off from the airport. Andrea's stove seemed to me to belong to the same category.

Though I didn't mind its sophistication, its height was truly intimidating. American kitchens are designed for the average height of American women. I'm, eh, slightly shorter than that average. To give you an idea, objects placed on a middle or top shelf instantly become untouchables.

Decades before, to curb my irresistible urge to flee the kitchen, where my height is a major problem, Sam had made me a three-inch-high wooden step stool (covered with carpet, no less). It worked wonders. However, I could have kicked myself for not thinking to bring it with me to Andrea's.

But even if I had, it wouldn't have been nearly high enough for her stove. Viking gas ranges were obviously designed for restaurant chefs, or perhaps even the Vikings themselves, those tall and mighty Scandinavian pirates of the eighth century. I found a regular step stool to stand on instead. That licked the height handicap all right, but unfortunately, it brought on troubles of a different sort: the ten-inch stool was more than three times the height of mine at home. When I came off the stool, my feet anticipated three inches and fell into a void instead. Getting onto the stool, I'd miss the top and trip on it, spilling whatever was in my hand…

And if there were a word to sum up the utensils and everything else in that kitchen, it was *heavy*. I had to strain to raise a two-pound platter with my left hand, while my right hand wielded a spatula to my eyebrows, my feet on tippy toes, and my neck sticking way out. Every task in Andrea's kitchen seemed to say *Enough already*.

§

My problems in the kitchen, however, were trivial compared to the crisis the new parents were facing at the front lines. Following an occasional successful feeding, with her eyes half-closed and fingers curled, Sylvia was the picture of contentment, an angel in miniature. Unfortunately, those moments became more and more rare, to the point of being nonexistent.

The Chinese describe using one's last reserve of strength as *milk-sucking energy*. Sucking milk clearly is a strenuous activity, especially when both participants are rookies. Having had nine extra days to grow before making her appearance, Sylvia was not a small infant, and her appetite not exactly dainty. When supply and demand of mother's milk developed a serious gap, it was difficult to talk her into exercising patience.

The poor baby was hungry and cried day and night, while her parents were getting desperate. They couldn't eat or sleep, visiting daily the pediatrician and the lactation consultant (another profession I had never heard of) only to receive increasingly bad news: the baby had lost one-fifth of her birth weight, and she was running the risk of dehydration and jaundice.

I began to lose my cool.

I felt that if there was not enough breast milk, why not supplement it with formula, so that mother and baby could be spared suffering? Andrea had plenty of infant formula and baby bottles at home, courtesy of the hospital. Both she and Doug had been formula-fed. Though new medical research showed that mother's milk is far superior, there is nothing absolute in this world.

As my feelings about the situation grew stronger each day, I struggled to keep the words inside.

I cautioned myself that in American culture, youths seldom looked for advice from the previous generation. This was partly due to the fact that, in modern life, knowledge and experience of the elders can turn obsolete in no time. But it was also a cultural difference. Our kids were raised in American society and were much more independent, confident, and entitled than Sam and I were. As they got older, we increasingly had the feeling we were treading on thin ice. The things we said or did, benign and perfectly acceptable in the Chinese culture, could be perceived as controlling, lacking in trust, or passive-aggressive from the American perspective.

A Chinese friend once told me that every time she saw her daughter and family off after a visit, in addition to saying goodbye, she used to add, "Drive carefully." But a glimpse from the corner of her eye showed that her Caucasian son-in-law was offended. She wondered, *Did I say something wrong?*

One day she suddenly realized that, though she meant "Drive carefully" the way the Chinese say "Walk slowly," to express that they care and are sad to say goodbye, perhaps her son-in-law thought that she was accusing him of driving carelessly. She changed to "Have a nice trip" instead.

She complained to me, "I know when you're in Rome, you do what the Romans do, and the idea of a *nice* trip does include a *safe* trip. But I always feel this expression is too cold. It sounds like something you say to mere acquaintances, not family. I feel uncomfortable saying it to them, but oddly, it makes them happy..."

I didn't know what to say. I told her Clif was the first to teach me the formidable word *boundary*. There's the boundary between countries, of course. In America, however, there's also the boundary between people, something you don't cross, even in relationships as close as parent and child, husband and wife.

There are personal boundaries in China, too, but they are strictly hierarchical. Children must respect boundaries as far as their parents are concerned, but never vice versa.

Whatever a child does for her parents is part of her obligation; no expression of appreciation is necessary. For example, as much as I always bent over backwards to try to please my parents, I'd never once heard them say "thank you."

For those of us who grew up as children in China and became parents in America, we have had a long and rough road to traverse, from one extreme to the other. And we certainly got the short end of the stick.

I had to remind myself of these cultural and generational realities when breastfeeding became increasingly stressful for Andrea. With neither knowledge nor experience about natural childbirth or breastfeeding, I knew I wasn't qualified to weigh in. I was there to provide food, not opinion.

Andrea and Doug had probably encountered very few problems they couldn't solve, or difficulties they couldn't overcome. Faced with a goal that had such crucial ramifications to their baby's health, they went all out to succeed, as they did with all other challenges.

They were fighting for their daughter, but *I* was worried about *my* daughter as well. Andrea had caught a cold before going to the hospital, and the stress of giving birth only worsened her condition. She couldn't stop coughing. Devoting all her effort to breastfeeding, she couldn't eat or sleep, which, in turn, affected milk production—a vicious circle.

Perhaps it was due to the fact that I hadn't read any of the books on breastfeeding, and therefore couldn't appreciate its importance. Perhaps I lacked the American youthful can-do attitude. After all, I'm my father's daughter—my father, who snuffed any sprout of hope in me when he forbade me to study literature and be a writer. Though from the ashes, my inextinguishable wish eventually did enable me to write, I still acquiesce easily when confronted by obstacles. I'm too ready to compromise, to make do, even to give up.

But in this instance, I didn't see it as giving up, but simply giving what was needed; I threw caution to the wind and crossed the boundary by suggesting Andrea and Doug give the baby a bottle.

Initially, my suggestion was rejected outright because, once the baby was fed formula, it would be extremely difficult to get her to breastfeed.

Fortunately, however, in the end everyone did *give in* and bend to Sylvia's urgent need to feed. After six days, the lactation consultant decided it was time to supplement breast milk with infant formula.

Hallelujah!

§

After days on end spent cooking in Andrea's kitchen, I returned to San Diego. By then, however, my kitchen phobia was off the charts. We ate out every day for two weeks straight before I set foot in the kitchen again.

Looking back, I can see *zuoyuezi* was less of a resounding success. The new parents liked my food all right, but under the trying circumstances, it was irrelevant from day one.

Though I managed to survive my daughter's kitchen, learning to navigate the formidable cultural and generational gaps, *and* loving and abiding one another despite the huge gulfs, has remained our lifelong lesson.

Afterword

Whenever I write about my life, the first person who comes to my mind is my father. Without question, he has had the biggest impact on every facet of my life.

Only in my old age, alas, have I finally come to understand that my father was a textbook case of a narcissist. He had a larger-than-life personality that attracted admiration from everyone—except his family. He seemed to have everything going for him except self-knowledge. With his limited worldview, he dictated over his wife, children, and extended family, never paying any consideration to how we felt or what we wanted. He judged me from early childhood to be unlovable and unworthy, and I believed him implicitly; even to this day, more than two decades after his death, sometimes I find myself powerless to shake his opinion of me.

It was my father's narcissism and lifelong fear of Communism that landed me in this country. He sent his children to establish our lives in the new world, so that he and my mother could eventually join us.

To be an immigrant is to exist in a dark and lonely crevice between two unyielding, formidable cultures. My life seems to be forever in limbo. On the one hand, I can't entirely embrace the world I'm living in; on the other, I can't disavow everything in the world I came from.

I have grown accustomed to being invisible. I cultivate a double personality. It can be challenging and painful to live as a perpetual misfit, always looking in from the outside. Even now, in a senior living center where all the residents share the same fate, where we are all wounded soldiers on the great battlefield of age, I'm still an outsider, living apart from others in more ways than one.

Life as an immigrant has been more complicated than I could have anticipated or imagined, yet also far more enriching. Inevitably, I look at everything through the prism of two rather divergent cultures, and the result is my own eclectic perspective. When the choices for me are difficult, when I seem to be caught between the worst of both worlds, the situation offers, nevertheless, the benefit of making me think. My ultimate reward is the freedom to choose.

In other words, as much as my early upbringing would allow, my immigrant experience has afforded me the opportunity to be my own person. For this, I feel incredibly fortunate. For this, I gladly and gratefully pay the price, including that on (as Confucius would say), the most basic of human needs—food.

Acknowledgments

Throughout the process of writing this volume, my children have remained my most faithful and fervent supporters. I have greatly benefitted from discussions with them and I can always count on their help in solving my computer problems. In addition, Clif read the most challenging chapter of the book, and Andrea, despite her impossibly demanding schedule, set aside time to review the whole manuscript. Both offered invaluable suggestions.

I've been exceedingly fortunate to have a dream team of Elizabeth Norwood as my editor and Heidi Reed as my book designer, both of whom worked on my previous volume, *Under the Towering Tree: A Daughter's Memoir*. Liz again played the most indispensable role, tirelessly—shall I say, mercilessly—challenging me on points large and small. This book wouldn't be the same without her. Heidi again astonished me with her excellent and expeditious work and, most of all, her unerring aesthetic judgment.

I am enormously grateful to Anne Standley for volunteering to read the manuscript and for recommending me to WHYY, the Philadelphia station of NPR (National Public Radio), as a contributing blogger. Her interest in the manuscript and WHYY's publication of four of my essays (including three chapters of this book) provided vital encouragement.

Lastly, I owe a special debt to Barbara Felton, whose warm caring and treatment, using Donna Eden's energy medicine practices, rescued me from a recent health setback and kept me in sufficiently good condition to finish this book.

Made in the USA
Middletown, DE
14 January 2018